Life Skills for Boys

100 Things Every Boy Should Know How to Do to Impress a Girl (and Everyone Else!)

Table of Contents

Introduction Letter to Parents

Dear Parents,

Thanks for picking this book up for your son.

As your son transitions from being a child to an adolescent, he will start settling into his unique identity. These early years play a crucial role in him becoming a functional and productive teenager. Giving your son enough space to explore his identity can be difficult, but independence only comes from practice. He can no longer be attached to your hip and will need to navigate school and events on his own. As much as your guidance is needed in these formative years, allowing him to freely discover himself is also essential.

This book will teach your son the social, emotional, psychological, and physical skills they need to blossom into the successful person you want him to be. This journey of self-discovery and growth will be difficult – with many peaks and valleys – but at the same time, it can be a fulfilling time for you both. Have patience and commitment, and you will see the results manifesting in a well-adjusted and social young man!

Introduction Letter to a Young Man

Dear Young Man,

You are now starting a new chapter in life and becoming more independent. You are no longer a small child – and you're growing up fast! This means you will have to learn new skills to help you become a better person and connect with others.

This book will help you build confidence and teach you about new responsibilities. The world can be a difficult place with many ups and downs. The following chapters can equip you with the tools you need to overcome the challenges coming your way and strengthen you mentally.

From dealing with money to making friends and controlling your emotions, you will be given the tools to do more tasks on your own without looking to adults for help. You will learn how to be better at school, express yourself to your family and friends, and help out around the house.

You will have endless fun while exploring all the different advice that this book provides. Remember that your parents and other loved ones will always be there to help you, but this always remains your journey; remember kindness and compassion as you embark on it!

Section 1: Personal Care

Ever noticed how your favorite sports star or video game hero always looks sharp? It's not just about the jersey or the gear. Taking care of yourself is like unlocking a secret level in real life. It's about more than just smelling good; it's about feeling confident, staying healthy, and making a great impression on everyone you meet (especially those awesome girls you might have your eye on).

Think about it: when you feel good about yourself, you walk taller, smile wider, and tackle challenges with more energy. Personal care helps you be the best version of yourself. Furthermore, good hygiene habits can help you avoid getting sick, keeping you in top form for school, sports, and hanging out with friends.

Personal care covers a range of practices and habits essential for overall well-being. It plays an important role in promoting health, boosting self-esteem, and making positive social interactions easier. Here are just a few benefits of mastering personal care:

Health: Good personal care practices are directly linked to physical health. Maintaining personal hygiene, such as regular bathing, brushing teeth, and washing hands, helps prevent the spread of germs and lowers your risk of getting sick. Proper nutrition, exercise, and enough sleep are also a part of personal care that contribute to better health. Learning these habits from a young age establishes a foundation for a healthy lifestyle that can last a lifetime.

Good personal care practices are directly linked to physical health.[1]

Self-Esteem: Personal care makes a big difference when it comes to self-esteem and self-confidence. Those who look and feel clean and well-groomed are more likely to feel good about themselves. This positive self-image can boost your confidence and resilience (your ability to bounce back from things), allowing you to navigate life's challenges with a greater sense of self-assuredness.

On the other hand, neglecting personal care can lead to insecurity and low self-esteem, which may affect your personal and social life – at home and at school.

Social Interactions: Good personal care practices are vital for successful social interactions. Maintaining hygiene, dressing appropriately, and grooming yourself well can help you make positive first impressions. People are naturally drawn to those who appear well-kept and clean. Additionally, practicing good personal care shows respect for oneself and others, fostering better relationships and communication skills.

Mental Health: Taking care of yourself isn't just about your body. It's also about looking after your feelings and dealing with stress. Learning to handle how you feel and what stresses you out is a super important part of taking care of yourself. Using cool tricks like mindfulness, which is a way to calm your mind, and knowing when to ask for help can make you feel a lot better inside.

Independence: As you get older, being able to take care of yourself is really important. Learning personal care skills means you can do more things on your own. This helps you be ready to handle things by yourself, whether it's at school or later when you're grown up.

Preparation for Future Roles: Good personal care is a big deal for when you grow up. Keeping yourself neat and acting polite is important whether you're just hanging out or in a serious work situation. The habits you start when you're young will help you be ready for adult life.

Respect for Others: Personal care isn't just about keeping yourself clean and neat; it's also about being considerate of other people. When you take good care of yourself, you're also showing respect to those around you. This helps everyone feel comfortable and shows that you care about the community.

1. Grooming Essentials

Have you ever seen a guy who just looks put together? Like he's ready for anything – a game of hoops, hanging out with friends, or even a class presentation? That's what we call a well-groomed appearance. It's all about taking care of yourself and showing that you care about how you look. It signals confidence and gets you ready to tackle whatever the day throws your way.

Here's the breakdown of what makes a guy look sharp:

Hair

Clean and Neat: Your hair is one of the first things people notice. Keep it clean and looking its best by washing it regularly with shampoo and conditioner to get rid of dirt and grime. Ask a parent or barber to help you find the right shampoo for your hair type.

Style Points: Find a hairstyle you like – and one that's easy to take care of. Maybe it's a short, sporty cut, or maybe you like to wear it a little longer. Use a comb or brush to keep your hair looking neat, and if you want, try a little bit of hair gel to keep it in place.

Trim Time: Regular haircuts keep your hair looking healthy and neat. Ask your parents how often you should get a haircut.

Face

Clean and Clear: Your face is your introduction to the world. Wash it twice a day with soap and water to get rid of dirt and oil.

Smooth Moves: If you start to get pimples (and most guys do!), don't worry. Talk to a parent or doctor about finding a face wash made for guys your age to help keep your skin clear.

Nails: Trim and Terrific

Short and Sweet: Keep your fingernails and toenails trimmed short. Use nail clippers to cut them straight across, and make sure to clean under your nails with a nail brush when you wash your hands.

No Biting Zone: Biting your nails is a bad habit that can spread germs. So keep those fingers away from your mouth!

Clothes

Clean and Fresh: You wouldn't wear a dirty uniform to a game, so make sure your clothes are clean and fresh, too. Ask your parents to help you do laundry so you always have clean clothes to wear.

Fit Check: Clothes that fit well make you look and feel your best. Make sure your clothes aren't too big or too small.

Wrinkle-Free Wins: Wrinkled clothes look sloppy. Ask a parent or older sibling to show you how to iron or steam your clothes to keep them looking sharp.

Shoes:

Clean Kicks: Your shoes are your partners in adventure. Keep them clean by wiping them down with a damp cloth or brush.

Laced Up: Make sure your shoelaces are tied neatly.

The Total Package

Smell Fantastic: You want to smell fresh and clean, just like after a shower. Use deodorant every day, especially after gym class or playing sports.

Stand Tall: Good posture makes you look more confident and ready for anything. Stand up straight and pull your shoulders back.

Smile Strong: A genuine smile shows your personality and brightens up your face. Brush your teeth twice a day and take care of your smile to keep it sparkling.

Remember: Looking sharp isn't about being perfect; it's about showing that you take pride in yourself and your appearance. It's about feeling confident and ready to take on the world.

Grooming isn't just about sticking to a routine; it's super important for keeping you healthy, too! It helps get rid of germs and dirt that can make you sick. Plus, it keeps your skin soft and stops pimples and stuff like dandruff in your hair.

When you take good care of how you look, you feel better about yourself. This helps you feel more confident, which means you'll make a great impression when you meet new friends or even later when you're working as an adult. Being well-groomed helps others see you in a positive way and can help you succeed in lots of different areas.

Grooming helps with lots of things: keeping you healthy, making you feel good about yourself, helping you do well in life, showing your style, making you comfy, showing respect to others, and fitting in with different groups.

Now that you know why grooming is so cool, here are some ways you can take care of yourself every day.

Haircare

A good haircut that suits your face shape is key. Talk to your barber or stylist about what kind of cut would look best on you. They can help you choose a style that complements your features and is easy to maintain. Keep your hair clean by washing it regularly with shampoo and conditioner. If your hair is getting longer, consider using a little hair gel or wax to keep it neat. You can ask a barber or stylist for tips on how to style your hair.

Skincare

Depending on your preferences and skin type, you can use soap, face wash, or products like skin cleansers, toners, and scrubs to keep your skin clean and glowing. After washing your face, don't forget to apply moisturizer to keep the skin soft and prevent dryness.

Facial Hair Management (If Applicable)

When you hit puberty, you'll notice hair growing in your armpits, pubic, and facial areas. In that case, you must trim this hair to maintain cleanliness. Always use a clean razor and shaving cream to shave safely. Ask an adult for help at first.

Nail Care

Keep your nails short and clean. Trim them regularly, straight across, using nail clippers. Use a nail brush to remove dirt from under your nails. You can also use a nail file to smooth out any rough edges.

Proper Use of Deodorant

Deodorant or antiperspirant is your best friend. Apply it daily, especially after gym class or playing sports. Roll-on or stick deodorants are easy to use and less messy than sprays. Antiperspirant helps reduce sweating, while deodorant helps mask body odor.

Using Cologne

A little goes a long way. Apply cologne sparingly on pulse points like wrists or neck, as applying it on a warm area intensifies the scent and increases longevity.

Eyebrow Grooming

If you have bushy eyebrows, trim them with scissors. However, be careful not to cut too much. You can ask a family member for help if you don't know how to do it.

Use Skincare Products

Always use sunscreen to protect against the sun's harmful UV rays. If you live in an area with intense sun, use sunscreen with an SPF rating over 30.

2. Bathing and Showering

Regular bathing and showering are essential ways to keep the body clean. Use soap or a body wash, and don't forget to pay attention to areas like the feet, armpits, and neck.

Use Bath Accessories

Don't forget to exfoliate your skin (exfoliation removes dirt and dead skin) using a loofah or a washcloth. After applying soap, body wash, or body scrub, use the loofah gently; avoid scrubbing too hard to avoid irritating your skin.

3. Oral Hygiene

Brushing Teeth Properly

Dentists recommend using fluoride toothpaste and a soft-bristled brush to keep your teeth in great shape. But having the tools isn't enough; you should brush for at least two minutes and make sure that the brush reaches every tooth surface. Keep a steady speed and avoid brushing too hard, as this can easily damage the enamel and gums.

Hold your toothbrush at a 45-degree angle to your gums and brush in gentle, circular motions. Be sure to brush the outer, inner, and chewing surfaces of each tooth. Don't forget to brush along your gumline, where plaque and food particles tend to build up.

Gently brush your tongue to remove bacteria that cause bad breath. You can use your toothbrush or a tongue scraper. Start at the back of your tongue and work your way forward.

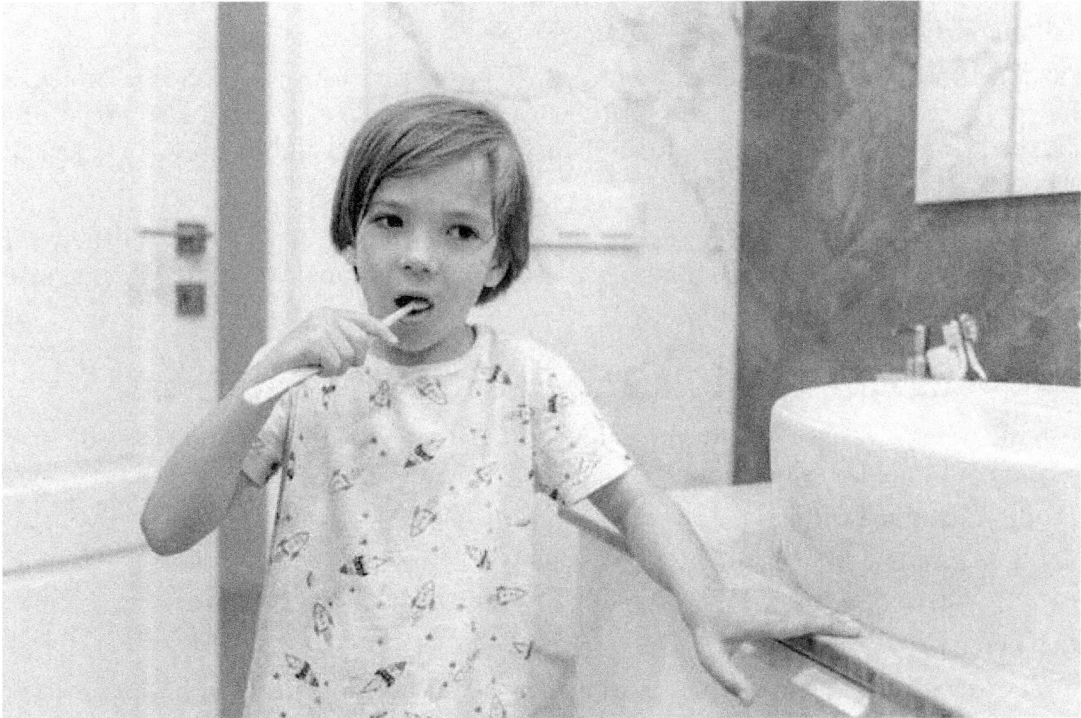

You should brush for at least two minutes and make sure that the brush reaches every tooth surface.[2]

Most brushes have a tongue cleaner, which you can use to clean the tongue and reduce bad breath. Rinse your toothbrush after each use and replace it every 3-4 months or sooner if the bristles are frayed.

Flossing

Flossing cleans places that your toothbrush can't reach. Ask an adult to show you how to floss the right way, using a gentle sawing motion to move the floss between your teeth. Curve the floss around the base of each tooth and gently slide it up and down beneath the gumline.

Make it a habit to floss once a day, *preferably before bedtime.*

Using Mouthwash

Gargle a small amount of mouthwash for 30 seconds and spit it out. Mouthwash has chemicals that prevent the growth of bacteria and keep the breath fresh.

Visiting the Dentist

Even if you don't have an active dental issue, visiting the dentist at least every six months is recommended. They will perform a complete oral cavity checkup, check for anomalies and cavities, and make sure that your teeth and gums are healthy. Your parents will probably make sure you don't miss appointments!

Recognizing Dental Problems

Bleeding gums, toothache, or cold or hot foods are causing pain. Those are signs of a dental problem. If you notice any of these signs, tell your parents or guardian right away and go see your dentist.

Teeth Whitening Safety

Never use teeth whitening products without your dentist's permission first. Some can be harmful or harsh. Likewise, avoid using DIY remedies for teeth whitening – like something you read on Facebook or Reddit or heard from a friend – as they can damage tooth enamel and increase teeth sensitivity.

Dental Emergency Preparedness

Besides knowing about the possible signs of tooth problems, you have to immediately inform your parents if you have a dental injury like a knocked-out tooth. Accidents and dental emergencies like this need to be taken care of by your dentist.

4. Toilet Habits and Bathroom Cleanliness

Always flush the toilet after use and avoid wasting toilet paper. Wash your hands for at least 20 seconds using soap and pat them dry using a towel.

Using Toilet Cleaning Products

Learning how to use toilet cleaning products safely is another skill to add to your arsenal. Organize the cleaning supplies and keep the bathroom tidy by putting each item away after use.

Avoiding Toilet Clogs

While minor clogs can be cleared using a plunger, avoid flushing anything besides toilet paper. No scraps of paper, no toys, etc.

Privacy in Shared Bathrooms

Be considerate of others when using shared bathrooms. Give them privacy and maintain cleanliness. When using public restrooms, be responsible and leave them clean. Always wash your hands thoroughly after using public restrooms.

5. Skin, Hair, and Dental Self-Examinations

Skin Self-Examination

Always check your skin for color changes, red spots, or an excessive number of moles. If you notice anything unusual, it's best to inform your parents or guardian so they can take you to the doctor. Some signs like dry skin, itching, redness, and rashes are mostly due to allergies or skin-related conditions. A visit to a dermatologist (a skin doctor) is necessary if these signs are persistent.

While you may have to go to the doctor if you find any skin changes, those minor cuts or scrapes can be easily treated at home. All you need to do is clean the wound, apply a small amount of antiseptic cream, and cover it with a bandage.

Once a month, take a few minutes to look over your skin in a well-lit room. Use a mirror to check areas you can't see easily, like your back, shoulders, and the back of your neck. Look for any new moles, freckles, or changes in the color or texture of your skin.

Pay attention to any spots that are:

- **Asymmetrical:** One half of the mole or spot doesn't match the other.
- **Border Irregularity:** The edges are ragged, notched, or blurred.
- **Color Variation:** The color is uneven, with shades of black, brown, tan, white, red, or blue.
- **Diameter:** The spot is larger than a pencil eraser (about 6 millimeters).
- **Evolving:** The mole or spot changes in size, shape, or color.

If you notice anything unusual, don't panic, but do tell a parent or doctor. They can take a look and determine if you need to see a dermatologist for further evaluation.

Hair and Scalp Self-Examination

While washing your hair, check your scalp for any unusual dryness, flakiness, or sores. Look for any redness, bumps, or patches of hair loss. If you see anything that concerns you, let a parent or doctor know.

Dental Self-Examination

When you brush your teeth, take a look inside your mouth. Check for any sores, redness, or swelling on your tongue, cheeks, lips, or gums. Also, look at your gums – they should be pink and firm, not red or swollen. If you notice anything unusual, tell an adult.

6. Dressing for Different Occasions

Understanding Dress Codes

Different occasions call for different outfits, whether it's a school event, a birthday party at your friend's house, or an outdoor adventure with family. If you are going to your school's debate competition, wearing a formal dress like a suit will be appreciated. Dress codes are followed to show respect for the occasion and the people involved.

Matching Colors and Patterns

Mixing colors and patterns can be fun, but knowing what looks good together is important. You can learn about color combinations and which patterns complement each other over time. Moms are usually a great resource to learn about fashion and what works – and what doesn't!

Shoe Choice

The type of shoes you wear depends on the activity. Sneakers are great for sports, while formal shoes are better for special events. Wearing the right footwear keeps you presentable, safe, and comfortable.

Dressing Independently

As you grew from a small child, you learned to dress yourself – buttoning shirts, zipping up jackets, and tying shoelaces. Now, you can learn to tie your ties (you might even like bowties sometimes!), choose belts, and create your own style.

Diet and Nutrition

Balanced Diet

A balanced diet means eating a variety of foods, including fruits, vegetables, grains, protein, and dairy. Each food group provides you with essential nutrients.

Portion Control

Learn about portion sizes from an adult. It's one of the best ways to keep yourself from overeating. To remember easily, use visual cues like your hand to estimate portion sizes.

Healthy Snacking

Snacking can be healthy if you choose nutritious options like fruits, vegetables, yogurt, or nuts. Doing it right can keep your energy levels up between meals. On the other hand, avoid munching too much on snacks as most packaged foods are low in nutrition.

Hydration

Water is crucial for your health. Drink plenty of it throughout the day to stay hydrated. Avoid sugary drinks like soda and limit how much juice you drink, as juices contain a lot of sugar!

7. Exercise and Fitness

Physical Activity

Being active is vital for your health. It can be sports, playing outside, or organized exercise. Find activities you enjoy, making exercise a fun part of your routine.

Benefits of Exercise

Exercise makes your body strong and healthy. It also improves your mood and helps you sleep better. Regular exercise is the key to leading a healthy life.

Staying Active

Keep moving throughout the day, even if it's not structured exercise. Walk, run, play, and participate in sports to stay active and fit.

Proper Warm-Up and Cool-Down

Before you exercise, warm up your muscles with stretches and light movements. After exercise, cool down with gentle stretches to prevent injuries.

Setting Fitness Goals

Setting goals helps you track your progress and stay motivated. Whether it's improving your running time or doing more push-ups, goals give you something to work towards.

8. Time Management and Organization

Daily Schedule

Create a daily routine to effectively manage your time. Include time for homework, chores, play, and relaxation.

Use a Planner or Calendar

Planners or calendars help you remember important dates and deadlines. Write down assignments, appointments, and activities to stay organized.

Planners or calendars help you remember important dates and deadlines.[3]

Prioritizing Tasks

Learn to prioritize tasks by importance and deadlines. Complete important and urgent tasks first. This helps you manage your time efficiently.

Organization Skills

To reduce clutter and distractions, keep your room, study area, and school supplies organized. An organized space makes it easier to focus and be productive.

Setting Goals

Set goals for your schoolwork, hobbies, and personal development. Goals give you direction and motivate you to work towards your dreams.

9. Communication and Social Skills

Active Listening

Active listening means giving your full attention when someone is speaking. Show your engagement by making eye contact, nodding, and asking questions.

Speaking Clearly

Practice speaking clearly and confidently so others can understand you. Good communication is critical to expressing your thoughts and ideas effectively.

Empathy

Empathy means understanding and caring about others' feelings and perspectives. Be a good friend by showing empathy when someone is upset or is going through a tough time.

Conflict Resolution

Conflicts happen, but it's essential to resolve them peacefully and respectfully. Talk calmly, listen to each other, and find compromises to solve disagreements.

Social Etiquette

Learn basic social etiquette, like saying "please" and "thank you," introducing yourself politely, and respecting personal space. Good manners help you make a positive impression on others.

Respecting Personal Space and Boundaries

Just like you have your space, other people have theirs too. It's important to respect personal boundaries to show others that you care about their feelings and comfort.

Don't Touch Without Asking

Always ask before touching someone else's body or belongings. This includes things like hugging, high-fiving, or borrowing something. Some people might not like to be touched, and it's important to respect their wishes.

Respect Personal Space

Give people space when they need it. Don't crowd them or invade their personal bubble. Everyone has a different comfort level with personal space, so pay attention to how people are reacting.

Ask for Consent

If you want to do something that involves someone else's body, always ask for their permission first. This includes things like playing tag, etc. If they say no, respect their decision.

Listen to Their Body Language

Pay attention to how people are reacting. If they seem uncomfortable or are trying to move away, respect their wishes and give them space. Even if they don't say anything, their body language can tell you a lot about how they're feeling.

The skills outlined in these sections include tools that will equip you with everything you need for personal care. From dressing appropriately for various occasions to understanding the importance of a balanced diet and staying active, these skills lay the foundation for a healthy and confident life. Effective time management and organization ensure that you can juggle your responsibilities without spending too much time on one thing – or too little on another.

Meanwhile, communication and social skills enable you to navigate social interactions, resolve conflicts, and build positive relationships with others. These life skills empower you with the knowledge and abilities to take charge of your care, physical well-being, and social interactions as you grow and face life's challenges with lots of confidence!

Section 2: Building Bonds - Communication

When you want to impress people, you must know how to communicate properly. By expressing yourself, you can find out what people want and help them understand you. Although some people are naturally good at communicating, it is a skill that can be learned with some practice.

Communication involves the words you say, the tone of voice you are using, and how you move your body. What you say and how you say it affects how people will treat you. Being careful of the way you communicate and building the skills to express exactly what you mean are brilliant ways for people to get to know you.

There are virtually endless different ways you can communicate. Your body language, tone of voice, and the words you use are all a part of communication. You cannot speak to your teachers or parents like you talk to your friends. You also cannot talk to strangers like you would speak to someone you've known for many years. Learning these differences and how people receive the message you send while you talk or text will help you have a lot more success in getting people to like you.

Active Listening

Have you ever felt as if even though you were in the middle of a conversation with someone, it felt like they weren't really listening? It's like when your parents were on the phone texting somebody, and they just nodded to whatever you said, but deep down, you knew they weren't listening. It does not feel great when someone pretends that they are listening to you. Sometimes, people listen to reply instead of listening to understand. Becoming a better listener means that you should not just listen to answer somebody, but you should make an effort to understand their words.

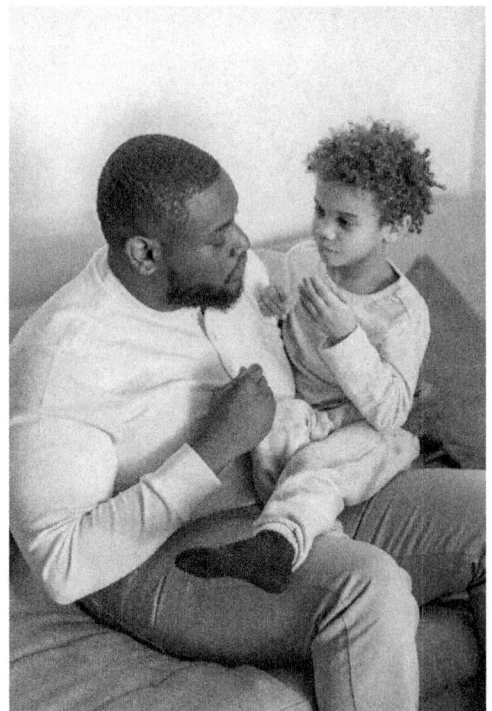

Active listening is when you listen carefully to what a person is saying and really think about their words before you reply.[4]

Active listening is when you listen carefully to what a person is saying and really think about their words before you reply. Even grownups do not know how to listen well sometimes.

10. How to Listen

- Look into the person's eyes. When you make eye contact with someone, it helps you focus on what they are saying. Eye contact also shows the person that you find them interesting.

- Try not to interrupt. You will sometimes find yourself getting very excited about what someone is saying because you have a cool story to share as well. Avoid the urge to interrupt no matter how much pressure you feel to speak up. It can be seen as rude when you interrupt, even if you do not mean it. Before you reply, let the other person finish what they are saying.

- Ask questions so that you can learn more about the person or the topic they are speaking about. Showing interest in what someone is communicating by asking questions is a great way to start new relationships. Asking questions will also help you better understand what someone is saying.

- Repeat what the person is saying back to them. Repeating something you have heard helps your brain process it a little bit better. It also shows the other person that you are trying your best to understand them.

- Listen to get the full meaning. Sometimes, people do not say exactly what they mean because they might be scared, do not have the right words, or do not want to hurt your feelings. You have to look at their body language and listen to their tone of voice to work out exactly what they mean. For example, someone might say, "Do whatever you like!" out of anger when they clearly do not mean it.

11. Broken Telephone

The broken telephone game can help you listen more actively and is a fun way to make new friends. The game needs a big group of ten or more people. You can play it at school or at a party. One person thinks of a short sentence and then whispers it in someone's ear. The message is then whispered to the next person and is passed along from player to player. The last person who gets the message will say it out loud to see if it matches what the first person said. This game helps you pay attention and is an entertaining way to connect with people.

Effective Speaking

Are you talkative and outgoing, or are you a little bit shy? Either way, learning how to speak effectively can help you become a person everybody wants to be around. Besides body language, speaking is the main way that people communicate. If you want people to know what you like, what you want, and how you feel, the best way to get that across to them is by speaking clearly.

World leaders of companies and countries all know how to speak very well. That is because if you want people to respect you, you must know how to use your words like a tool. Words can either build people up and make them feel amazing or tear them down. The words you use and how you say them are powerful, so you must always be careful when it comes to what you say. Speaking effectively means using your words to get what you want, not hurting others, and encouraging them to be better people.

12. How to Speak to a Group

In life, you will need to speak in front of groups. It can be scary and make you nervous, but some tips will help you through it. Maybe you are at a party, at school, or at a sports event, and you would like to say something. The following steps can be used to ensure you are heard, and your words are taken seriously.

- **Know Who You Are Talking to.** Say you are speaking to a group of people who love video games but hate sports. Avoid talking about sports because they will not be able to relate. Having a good understanding of the type of people you are speaking to, what they like, and what they do not like will help you choose the right words. You have to change your words or even the way you speak depending on whom you are speaking to.

- **Practice Makes Perfect.** The more you speak in front of groups, the better you will become at it. You are a bright, shining light that has a lot to offer. Do not hide that. Let your unique personality shine through by speaking to groups whenever you feel that you need to.

- **Take Charge of a Space.** Don't sit in a corner by yourself when there is a group of new people around. You do not have to make yourself feel smaller and hide away from the crowd. How will people know how wonderful you are if you do not make yourself known?

- **Be Confident.** Confidence is when you believe that you have something great you want the world to see. Other people will not believe in you if you do not believe in yourself.

- **Have Fun.** Would you want to be around someone who looks miserable all the time? If you are enjoying yourself, people will want to be near you more. So, having fun with a group can help you be more impressive.

13. Be Brave!

Your thoughts and feelings matter. People in your life, whether friends or family, will sometimes try to convince you that you should not speak freely. You cannot allow people to take your voice away from you. If you are angry, happy, sad, or uncomfortable, do not bottle up your feelings. Express yourself so people can know how to talk to you. You cannot expect the world to read your mind. The only way other people will know what is happening in your head is if you speak up.

When you feel afraid to say what is on your mind, do not keep quiet and ignore your feelings. Take a few deep breaths and be courageous enough to say what's on your mind. You will sometimes think too much about how people will act if you say something, but you will never really know unless you let it out. If you do not like something or if you appreciate what someone does for you, let it be known by using your voice.

Body Language

What comes to mind when you think of communication? Most people think of communication as using words to send a message, whether it is through writing or speaking. Body language is the main way humans communicate. How you use your body when talking tells people a lot about what you are saying. Your emotions show on your body. When you are happy, you might smile or giggle. When you are excited, you might jump around. When you are angry, you will frown and clench your teeth.

Other than your facial expressions, can you think of other ways you use body language when speaking to people?

14. Maintain Good Posture

How you stand and hold your body says much about what is on your mind. You will look lost if you are slumped over, staring at your feet. When you hold your head up high, you appear to know exactly what is going on around you.

The way you stand and hold your body is called posture. For you to impress people, you need to have good posture. Make sure that when you sit or stand, your back is straight, your chest is out, and your head is held high. Think about your favorite superhero. When they come face to face with a powerful villain, they stand with their head held high to show that they have no fear. Keep your head up and look like a superhero.

15. Using Your Body to Communicate

Just as you use your words to tell people what is on your mind, you can use your body. When your parents are angry with you, you can see it in their bodies and their faces. Sometimes, when you are sad, it feels good when someone gives you a pat on the back or a hug. Touching people or using your hands and body to speak is how you can make communication feel more personal. Remember that you must have consent before you touch anybody.

What will you do with your hands if you want to communicate fear?

What can you do with your legs to make the story you are telling better?

When you use your whole body to communicate, it makes people pay attention and remember what you have said.[5]

Using your whole body to communicate makes people pay attention and remember what you have said. People use their eyes as much as their ears when listening to you. Your words must be tied to the right movements to get your point across. Remember that when you communicate with someone, you must think about how they will receive your words. Body language makes a person's listening experience interesting. If you want to be remembered even when you are not around, you need to make the right communication choices.

Respectful Disagreement

Have you ever had an argument with friends or family? It is normal to disagree with people. Everyone is unique and has their own thoughts and opinions. Sometimes, people will believe completely different things from you. Disagreements do not need to turn into fights. If you learn to disagree respectfully, your life can be much smoother.

16. Use Your Words

You might be disagreeing with someone that makes you so angry that you feel like hitting them. This behavior is unacceptable. It can be difficult to use your words when you get too angry. Walk away and count to thirty. Breathe slowly until you calm down, then come back to explain why you got angry. People have to make an effort to understand one another.

17. Be Willing to Listen

Nobody is right all the time, not even your parents. When you disagree with someone, you want your point to be heard. To be respectful, you must hear someone else out, too. You must give the respect you want to receive.

Try asking, "Why do you feel that way?" or "Why do you think that?"

You can also say, "I respect what you are saying, but I do not agree. This is what I think."

Conflict Resolution

Disagreements can get so out of hand that they turn into fights. Given that people live together and spend so much time with friends and family, disagreements are inevitable. When you have an argument at school or at home, you must find a solution that allows everyone to be happy and remain friends.

18. Conflict Resolution Strategies

Finding solutions for an argument or fight is called conflict resolution.

Here are four steps you can use to resolve an argument:

1. First, you need to stop and think about what you are saying or doing. Spending some time away from the person you are arguing with can help with this step.

2. Next, everyone involved in the argument must be given a chance to share their point of view without being interrupted.

3. After everyone has had their turn to talk, you and the person you are arguing with can think of positive ways to move forward so that both of you can be happy.

4. Suppose you cannot come to a solution everybody involved can agree with. In that case, it is best to respect your differences instead of trying to get someone to change their mind.

Effective Questioning

When you are first getting to know someone, the best way to connect with them is to ask a few questions. It can be difficult to ask the right questions, especially if you do not know one another. Learning how to ask the right things can help you quickly relate to new people. People love talking about themselves and the things they like doing, so asking questions allows them to open up to you. It also opens the door for them to ask you questions, so you also get a chance to express yourself.

19. Asking the Right Questions

To get someone to open up to you and become your friend, avoid asking yes or no questions. For example, you may like playing soccer, so you ask a new friend, "Do you like soccer?" The conversation will quickly end after they answer. You want to focus on asking open-ended questions to form bonds. Here are some examples:

- Who is your favorite superhero, and why do you like them?
- What is your favorite place to visit, and why do you like going there?
- What makes you angry or happy?
- What is your biggest fear and why?
- If you could do anything in the world, what would you do?

See how these do not have yes or no answers. These are the types of questions you should ask new people.

Section 3: Building Character

Time and again, the world has stressed the importance of building your character. They say that it is a reflection of your thoughts, a window to your soul. These poetic definitions don't really provide an insight into its meaning. Before you start building your character, you should know what it is in the first place.

Your character is a combination of qualities that make you YOU![6]

Your character is a combination of qualities that make you, well, *you*. They can be mental qualities like creativity, self-awareness, confidence, patience, intelligence, and so on. They can be regarding your moral inclinations (what you consider right and wrong), like compassion, integrity, humility, kindness, sense of justice, etc. Your character is also a blend of your thoughts and feelings and how you act on them.

No matter what you may hear, a person with a good character isn't always surrounded by good thoughts and feelings. They may think and feel all kinds of thoughts and feelings (the good and the bad), but they act according to the good side of their mental and moral states. These good actions are what make them have a good character.

Imagine your friend just got a new bike. You want to take it for a spin, but they propose a trade. You can ride their bike if you promise to let them play on your gaming console for a few days. You happily agree and ride it around the neighborhood through the evening. However, when it comes to fulfilling your part of the bargain, you suddenly have reservations. You will have to sacrifice some of your gaming time to let your friend play, and you don't feel entirely comfortable with that.

Despite your thoughts, are you willing to sacrifice your gaming time to let your friend play? If you do, that shows you have the makings of a good character. Did you decide not to fulfill your promise instead? That shows that your character is in the gray area somewhere, leaning towards bad. However, don't let one bad decision define your character.

To err is human, as they say. At your age, it's easy to make mistakes. If you take responsibility for those mistakes and learn from them, then you are showing good character.

For instance, when you didn't let your friend play with your game console, did you feel bad about it a little later? You don't have to keep feeling bad about it. Just go over to their house, apologize for not holding up your end, and invite them to play the next day.

Developing a good character is all about handling a series of such mistakes and decisions. It doesn't happen overnight. At your age, your character is malleable (flexible) and can be crafted into whatever you want it to be.

20. Self-Discovery

Self-discovery is the process of understanding your values, aspirations, goals, likes, dislikes, and everything in between. Your character is not built from scratch. It needs a foundation, something that already exists within you. Finding the bricks for laying this foundation is what self-discovery is all about. Go to someplace you won't be disturbed, take a few deep breaths to reach a sense of calm, and ask yourself the following questions to begin your journey of self-discovery:

- **How Are You Feeling Right Now?**

You will be asking these questions of your inner self. Don't just jump into the important questions. Make your inner self comfortable with yourself by asking how they are feeling. Your immediate answer may be "calm" or "okay". Probe further by asking what emotions you are going through. Sharing your emotions will eventually make your inner self more comfortable around you.

- **What Do You Want Right Now?**

Apply the same strategy as before. Look for your immediate reply and probe for a deeper answer. You may want to have some water right now, but if you think about it more, you may feel like wanting to get your homework done or play with your friends.

- **What Interests You?**

What are you passionate about? What moves you and motivates you? It could be your favorite movie or a school subject. Probe further by asking what interests you physically or emotionally. What piques your curiosity? What inspires your spirit?

• What Brings You Down?

What are your dislikes? Which subject do you hate? What kind of movie do you despise? What kind of games do you hate playing? What type of person makes you angry? Focus on unearthing your negative emotions.

• How Can You Reinforce Your Strengths and Work on Your Weaknesses?

Now that you have determined your problems, it's time to find their solutions. How can you use your strengths to achieve your goals? How can you take on your weaknesses in your own stride or maybe transform them into your strengths?

• What Are Your Values?

This is probably the most important question of them all. It will help you set your moral boundaries. How will you behave in society? Where do you draw the line between good and bad? What are your gray areas? Are you willing to let go of your values to achieve your goals?

As you grow older, your answers to these questions may change. Record your answers in a journal to keep track of your journey of self-discovery.

21. Self-Discipline

With self-discovery, you will realize your weaknesses. Self-discipline will teach you how to conquer them as you work to improve your strengths. It will pave the path to your goals and ambitions, teaching you ways to pull them out of your dreams and into an achievable real-world scenario.

• Reducing Distractions

Reducing distractions and focusing on the task at hand is the first step to improving self-discipline. Practice studying with a lot of distractions around you (say, study at a park in the evening). Try to block out those distractions and focus on your studies.

• Develop Goal-Friendly Habits

Do you want to become an astronomer? Go star-gazing every night. Try to read space books and encyclopedias for at least an hour each day.

• Let Go of Limiting Habits

Does playing games help you achieve your dreams? Reduce your daily playing time from a few hours down to an hour and, eventually, to no more than 15-20 minutes a day.

• Plan for Failure

Accept that failure is a part of life. No matter how hard you try, there is always a chance that you might fail. Plan for that eventuality. Don't think of failure as an unchartable ocean. Imagine it as a river you need to cross to reach your goal.

Reducing distractions and focusing on the task at hand is the first step to improving self-discipline.[7]

22. Accountability

Accountability is just another name for taking responsibility for your actions. Do you feel happy when your actions lead to success? Learn to feel happy when you make a mistake, too, because that will, in some way or other, lead to your success. Associate positive thoughts with your failures. Then, you will find it easier to take responsibility for a negative action.

Expand your horizons and be open to change. Accept the consequences (good or bad) of your actions. Take advice from the people around you, but don't blame them if things don't turn out as you hoped; after all, it was *your decision* to take their advice! Own up and move on.

23. Respect

Give respect to gain respect. How many times have you heard this? Still, something keeps you from giving respect to others. It's called *ego*. Ego can be beneficial if used wisely. It can build your confidence and make you more resilient. But more often than not, it gets in the way of respecting others.

Don't start off by assuming that you know more than most. Other people always have something to offer. Find it and respect them for it. For example, one of your classmates may not be good at sports, but they may always get straight A's in all their subjects. Learn to respect them for that instead of looking down on them during extracurricular activities. Here's a fun activity you can do to both give and gain respect.

Pick a classmate every day and try to figure out what they are good at. Then, during lunch, compliment them for it. They may simply thank you or give you a compliment in return. Either way, you will have earned their respect.

24. Gratitude and Appreciation

Ambition is an excellent trait, but only if you are happy about what you are blessed with. Gratitude is the act of being thankful for what you are and what you get. Did someone offer to share their sandwich with you, but you don't like sandwiches? Don't walk away or ignore them. They probably don't know your likes and dislikes. They offered you the sandwich simply out of the kindness of their heart. Show your gratitude by thanking them. You can also show your appreciation by sharing something from your lunch.

It's easy to overlook gratitude and appreciation in your day-to-day life. Before going to sleep, try to reflect on your day and write down all the things for which you are thankful. Show your gratitude to those people the next day.

25. Kindness

Kindness is the one quality that has the power to build your character all on its own.[8]

Kindness is the one quality that has the power to build your character all on its own. The kinder you are, the stronger your character will be. It is a trait that triumphs over all other traits. Your kindness contributes to the betterment of the world. It will not only boost your confidence but that of others as well. It has the capacity to have a substantial snowball effect.

For example, if you help a peer with their homework, there's a good chance they may help some other student in need. That student, in turn, will help a few others, and so on. Because of your kind act, someone you don't know may help you with your studies someday. Similarly, any unkind act also has a snowball effect. Now ask yourself this: Would you rather have people be kind to you than rude?

You can practice kindness by simply looking around as you go about your day and helping those in need. Help an elderly individual cross the road. Hold the door open for those who arrive in class just after you. Clean up after yourself at home. Help your parents with some of their simple chores. Indeed, with kindness, the possibilities are endless!

26. Rational Thinking

This may be a slightly difficult skill to acquire. Rational thinking is the ability to think and reason without your emotions getting in the way. Its basis lies in cold, hard facts that are verifiable down to a T. However, it doesn't mean that you shouldn't consider your emotions at all.

For instance, you catch one of the students cheating during the exams. You approach them and call them out on it. They apologize to you and assure you that it won't happen again. Rational thinking dictates that you should call them out on their cheating – tell the teacher. However, your emotions will prompt you to take their apology into consideration. Don't stop thinking rationally, though. Did the apology seem genuine? You may give them another chance and see if they make good on their promise.

Emotional thinking, on the other hand, is when you base your decisions entirely on emotions. Did you decide not to report the student just because you felt sorry for them? That will make it a bad decision. Did you report them anyway, just because you don't like them? Also, a bad decision. The fact of the matter is, embrace rational thinking, but don't ignore your emotions.

27. Keeping Promises

The sacredness of a promise may have been hammered into you from a very young age, either by your peers or by your parents. However, as you grow older, you may encounter certain situations when breaking a promise is acceptable. Imagine that you have promised to keep your friend's secrets no matter what. One fine day, they steal a pen from their classmate. You feel bound by your promise and don't say anything about it. A few days later, they steal another classmate's tablet, and before you know it, they have a whole hoard of stolen items in their backpack!

What if you had broken your promise and reported them the day they stole that pen? They may have hated you for it, but they would have been grateful over time. So, when exactly can you keep promises, and when can you break them? Here are a few tips that will help.

- Think twice before promising something. Can you fulfill that promise? Does it go against your morals? Does it have the capability to go against your morals in the future?
- Make sure the promise is realistic.
- Make sure the promise is specific. Don't be vague, like promising to keep all their secrets.
- Pick a good role model and learn from them. When do they keep or break their promises?

28. Apologize

An apology not only builds bridges but character, too. To apologize, you need to admit that you have made a mistake. To admit a mistake, it's important to know that it's okay to make mistakes. A simple "sorry" often works best, but a thoughtful apology works wonders.

1. State the reason for your apology. What was the mistake you made?
2. Let them know you understand your mistake. Own up to it.
3. Is there a reason why that mistake happened? State it, but don't make it sound like an excuse. Add something like, "This may be the reason, but I understand the fault is mine."
4. Assure them it won't happen again.
5. Say that you would like to make amends. For instance, if you mistakenly damaged their science project, you could offer to help mend it.

If you are finding it hard to say all these things in person, write them an apology letter, send them an apology card, or record your apology on video.

29. Forgive

When you have genuinely apologized to someone, what do you hope to hear back? Those three sweet words, "I forgive you," are bound to bring peace to your troubled heart. That is exactly what others hope to hear when they apologize to you. The point is that an apology isn't required for you to forgive someone. You can forgive them for your own good, too. How long are you going to hold a grudge? Forgiveness will lighten your burden. Don't let your ego get in the way of your happiness.

Look deep within yourself. How did the person offend you? Why are you still letting them affect you? Let them go. Let their actions be a thing of the past. Why should what they think about you bother you? Forgive them to free your heart from all the negativities. Forgive them *for your own sake.*

Section 4: Being a Good Friend

There are very few life skills as beneficial as cultivating and maintaining good friendships. People can survive without friends, but they cannot thrive. What's the point of surviving for the sake of it? Friendships provide meaning to your survival. They give you a reason to live, regardless of your goals and ambitions. Friendships teach valuable lessons in empathy, compromise, and effective communication. They help individuals learn to give and take, support and be supported. These relationships provide opportunities to respect differences and embrace diversity, encouraging personal growth.

Friendships teach valuable lessons in empathy, compromise, and effective communication.[9]

Having strong friendships is really good for your health. Scientists have found that people with lots of friends usually live longer, feel less stressed, and don't get sick as often. When you're going through a tough time, having friends to help and support you can make a big difference in feeling better.

Friendships also help make communities stronger by bringing people together, no matter how different they are. This helps everyone understand each other better and makes the world a kinder place.

However, not all friendships are good for you. Sometimes, some friends might make you feel bad or bring you down. These kinds of friends might seem fun when things are going well, like when you have a new video game to play, but they disappear when you really need help, like if you're dealing with bullies at school. It's important to choose friends who are there for you both in fun times and when you need support.

Signs of a Bad Friend

You don't want to end up with bad friends in life. Chances are, you will absorb their qualities and become a bad friend yourself. Here are a few signs to help you determine if you are becoming one:

• Distrust

A friend is nothing if not trustworthy. If you find it hard to trust your friends or vice versa, then it is a clear indication of an unhealthy friendship. Do they rarely, if ever, invite you to their house? Do they often hesitate before lending you anything? While playing a competitive game, do your own teammates keep watching their backs around you?

• Judgments

Do you tend to have an opinion about everything? Do you pass judgment over the smallest of things? Assume you don't like the clothes your friend is wearing. Do you start getting judgmental about those types of clothes, saying how they aren't fashionable? It's okay to be blunt with friends, but doing it excessively will only cause problems between you.

• Too Clingy

Friendships are for life, but they shouldn't constitute your whole world. Your friend has a world of their own that has nothing to do with you. Do you try to be with them every waking moment of their life? Do you tend to have constant sleepovers? In the initial stages of your friendship, you may feel like the two of you are inseparable, but as time goes on, you will both realize the importance of having your own space.

• Absenteeism

Is your friendship defined by your continual absences during important occasions? Are you only present during the good times? Conversely, do you only show up during bad times and emergencies? It might seem like a noble decision, but it's not the right one for maintaining your friendship.

As you grow up, you will come across many more signs of being a bad friend. If you display those signs, you may end up friendless for the rest of your life. It's a harrowing prospect. So, what are the signs of being a good friend? How can you become one?

30. Initiate New Friendships

Making new friends is all about meeting new people, making eye contact with them, starting a conversation, and finding common ground. Are you hesitant to do either or all of these things? You may have low self-esteem, and you probably just need a push. Here are a few good tips to get you started.

• Join a Club

School is a great place to meet new people, but you probably want to focus on your studies there. Join a club or a hobby group during your free time. You have already found common ground with the people there. You just need to start a conversation. Go over to them and ask why they joined the club, or talk to them about your interests until they open up.

• Help or Seek Help

Helping someone is the perfect way to start a friendship with them. They already know that you will be a good friend just because you helped. Gratitude can open the doors of friendship like no other.

If you cannot find anything to help them with, seek help instead. Go over to them and ask if they could help you with something. Don't just make something up. A friendship started on falsehood doesn't usually end well. Are you stuck with a homework problem? Having trouble finding a book in the library? Want to know different moves at a sports club?

• Practice Having an Open Body Language

Your body language speaks volumes about your sociability. Do you sit stiffly with your arms crossed? Do you often avoid eye contact with others? That may give them the impression that you are not friendly or approachable. Don't cross your arms, place your palms on your knees, and try to look around often. Don't hesitate to make eye contact with your peers. Give them a smile before looking away.

When you approach someone you want to be friends with, be as polite as possible. Ask "may" questions instead of asserting your authority. Show your interest in them with your facial expressions. Don't look at your phone while they are talking. If you've received an important message, apologize and excuse yourself before pulling out your phone.

31. Be a Good Listener

A good friend is always a good listener. Don't hesitate to share your joys and sorrows, but, more importantly, listen to what is being shared. People prefer good listeners over good talkers.

• Maintain Eye Contact and Open Posture

As discussed in the previous section, keep an open body language while listening. Don't just hear; show that you are listening. Maintain eye contact throughout, but don't stare. Display a few listening cues like a nod of understanding or a smile of encouragement.

• Interpret Non-verbal Cues

While talking, people often express themselves with their hands or facial expressions. At times, they may say one thing, but their non-verbal cues portray an entirely different emotion. Any incident can generate mixed emotions within people. For instance, they may be jokingly telling you how they fell from their bike, but they may have balled up their fists during the entire narration. That may imply that the incident still hurts them. In this case, you may laugh but also empathize.

• Avoid Interrupting

Imagine that you are engrossed in telling an interesting story from your past. How would you feel if someone interrupted you? It would completely derail your train of thought, and you may even lose interest entirely. While someone is sharing, don't interrupt them. If you want to ask questions or clear up doubts, wait for them to finish.

32. Trust and Honesty

Trust and honesty go hand in hand. There can't be one without the other. They are the building blocks of friendship. Your friends want to know your true self. If you aren't comfortable being around them, you're not good friends yet. If you want to be trustworthy enough for them to share every little thing with you, you need to share your heart with them. Take off the mask you show the world, and let your friends see the real you. That is the only way you will gain their trust.

- Be straightforward

- Dress not to impress but to be yourself

- Don't exaggerate or blow things out of proportion

- Speak the truth, even if it means hurting your friends

Once you have gained the trust of your friends, don't ever betray it. If you do, it won't take long for your friendship to end. Sadly, that won't be the only outcome. Betrayal may cause your friend to spiral. They may get into some really bad habits. It will also adversely affect their physical and mental health. The worst outcome is that they may never learn to trust anyone ever again.

33. Loyalty

Apart from honesty, you also need to be loyal to gain your friend's trust.[10]

Apart from honesty, you also need to be loyal to gain your friend's trust. Do you put their needs before your own? Can they depend on you when something goes wrong in their life? Never make them feel like they are a random part of your life. Your care for them should extend to their ideals and beliefs. Even if you don't agree with them, you should respect them. Loyalty is earned over time, so you should always be ready to show it when the need arises.

34. Should You Offer Advice?

When you begin a new friendship, you should never start off by offering advice. Just listen to what they have to say. Don't pass any judgments. Put yourself in their shoes. If you were going through the same thing, all you would want is someone to listen. Once you are good friends, then you may give advice freely, but within a limit. Nobody likes a know-it-all.

• When to Offer Advice

Try to follow this simple rule. Offer advice only when asked. Look for non-verbal cues. Does their talking sound like a plea for help? Are they too proud to ask for advice? If you know them well and understand their non-verbal cues, you may offer advice whenever you feel like they need it.

• When NOT to Offer Advice

Often, people dish out advice for their own selfish reasons. They just want to make themselves feel better. When you feel the urge to offer advice, stop and think for a moment. Are you doing it because it will benefit your friend, or do you have a hidden agenda? If it's for something other than benefiting your friend, don't give the advice.

After you do your part, let your friend be. Don't follow up by asking if they followed your advice. If they didn't, and something bad happened to them, don't gloat. Continue to support them and show them that you care.

35. Offer Support

Friendship is a joyride that makes the journey of life worth taking. It also acts as a crutch to help you keep walking despite the hurdles. Sit beside your friend on this joyride and be that crutch for them when they need it. Offer your support during the good times and the bad.

- Use your words. Tell them that you are there for them. Can't make it to their party? Tell them that you would have loved to be there, and let them know why you cannot. Are they going through a tragedy? Ask them what they need and assure them of your support through those hard times.

- Use your body language. Hold their hand (if they are a girl) or place your arm around their shoulders. Let your eyes do the talking. Give them an assuring look or a keen, interested stare.

36. Boundaries Matter

Boundaries in friendships aren't looming, impenetrable walls. They are like fences you can mend if need be. They help you see where the line is and make you understand that crossing it may cost you the friendship. You may like doing something, but your friend hates it. You can't just coerce them into doing it. It also doesn't mean that you should stop being friends. Set boundaries and define the following things:

- What you will and won't do while hanging out together
- What you will and won't share
- The part of their lives you should not ask about
- The qualities they value and despise

- How supportive you can be with each other
- The things they consider a definite "no"

37. Apology and Forgiveness

In friendships, mistakes are inevitable. You aren't perfect, and neither is your friend. Accept this fact; only then will you be able to forgive their mistakes.

Did they cross a boundary you set? Did they do something you didn't like, something you already stated several times you hated?

If they have really hurt you, a good friend will notice that and always apologize. Don't take too long to accept their apology and forgive them. Making up after a fight is one of the best parts of a friendship because it makes you realize how much you mean to each other.

If you make a mistake or hurt your friend's feelings, apologize immediately after. The longer the fight lasts, the larger the cracks will be, and the harder it will be to mend them.

38. Generosity

Friendship is about giving your all without expecting anything in return. It's unconditional love, a bond that transcends material needs. A good friend doesn't hesitate to be generous. Your friend will often be generous to you, too, until you both won't be able to keep score of each other's generosity.

It isn't always about material things, like letting them play your games or borrow from your book collection. Generosity can be mental – *and spiritual, too.* You can share your knowledge, lend them an ear, or teach them certain skills. Giving is a choice. Choose to believe in your friendship and trust in your friend. The rest will follow.

39. Integrity

In friendship, this quality is right up there, along with trust and honesty. In fact, without integrity, your friend cannot really trust you with anything. For example, if they have shared a secret with you, your integrity will stop you from sharing it with someone else. Without honor, you won't be able to acquire any of the skills above. You won't be able to meet your friend's expectations without integrity. All you have to do is be as honest as you can and honor as many of their commitments as possible. Feel free to joke around with the age-old concept of honor with friends, but when things get serious, use your integrity to strengthen your bond.

Section 5: Skills for Success

Being successful has nothing to do with luck. People who have reached the highest levels of success have worked very hard to get there. They also had to have the right life skills to get there. Learning the skills in the exercises below will help you develop the qualities you need to get good grades in school, perform well in after-school activities, work together with friends and classmates, and put you on the road to a bright future.

People who have reached the highest levels of success have worked very hard to get there.[11]

To succeed, you need to know how to use your time to the fullest, set goals, plan, adapt, and manage your stress. It is not easy to succeed, so you must put your all into everything you do. You also cannot allow yourself to be distracted by anything that does not add to your success. Every small choice you make adds up to big choices that will help or hurt you in the long run. That's why you must work on yourself every day to be the best person you can be.

With the right choices and commitment to your goals, success is definitely on the way! Although it will be difficult, it will also be fun. Nothing worth having comes easily. Your focus and the support you get from friends and family will help you achieve your dreams. Always work hard, and do not be afraid to ask for help. It is impossible to build success alone, so look to people who know better to show you the way while you always try your best.

Critical Thinking and Problem-Solving

Do you like asking a lot of questions and learning new things? It is great to ask questions because it gives you new facts that you never knew before. Sometimes, people lie or repeat things that they have previously been told.

People have different views about things in the world depending on where they came from or how they grew up. This means that many people have different opinions about what is right and wrong, how you are supposed to live, and what rules to follow.

Your parents and teachers tell you what you must do or what you should believe. As you grow up, many people will tell you a lot of different things about the world. Some of those things will be true, others will be false, and a few of them will just be a matter of what people prefer, like choosing a favorite color. Critical thinking is when you ask a lot of questions about new information to see if it is right. Critical thinking helps you make the right decisions in life and is a great way to find out what is true and what is the best way to solve problems.

40. Analyzing Situations

Sometimes, people have been doing the same thing the same way for many years. Someone new could come along and show them a better or faster way to do the same thing. Looking at an activity in different ways to find new solutions to problems is a big part of critical thinking.

- What is your favorite invention in the world?
- Can you think of ways that invention could be better?
- Draw a picture of how you would make your favorite invention better.
- Many people in the world do not have enough food to eat. Some people have more food than they need. Why do you think that is?
- Draw three different pictures of things you could do to make sure that everybody on earth has enough food to eat.

41. Systematic Problem Solving

Tiny problems, like when you lose a pencil and your friend lends you one, are easy to solve. Big problems are more difficult to handle. That's why when you have a bigger problem, you can use these steps to find the solution:

Step 1: Define the problem. Defining your problem is when you describe what your problem is. For example, you lose your pen, and you cannot write during a test.

Step 2: Describe what it would be like if the problem was solved. For example, you have the right pen to write a test.

Step 3: Break the problem up into smaller parts. A big problem can be difficult to think about, but when you break it down into smaller parts, you can think of a solution. For example, you might be a bad soccer player even though you love the sport.

Solving the problem of how to be a better soccer player is too difficult. So, you can break it up into learning how to kick the ball, to pass, to shoot, and to dribble. You can now tackle each smaller problem better, and that will add up to solving the bigger problem.

Step 4: Create a plan. Once you know what the problem is and you have broken it into smaller parts, you must create a plan to solve it. For example, you might be bad at dribbling in soccer, so you can make a plan to practice for thirty minutes every day.

Step 5: See if your plan is working. After thirty days, you can compare your current dribbling skills to when you started. If you have gotten better, you can carry on with your plan. If you haven't, you will need to change your plan.

Think of a problem you are struggling with at school or home.

Use the steps above to work out a way to solve that problem.

Time Management

Have you ever been having a lot of fun, and it felt like time was going by very quickly? People do not have enough time to do everything they want to do. That's why you need to use your time wisely.

If you have a school project, you cannot play video games all day and work on your project at the last minute. If you do that, your work will not be as good as it could have been. If you waste your time, you will also not be able to do all the things you love.

Using your time properly will give you a chance to do schoolwork and chores – and still have fun. If you manage your time, you will not get in trouble with your parents or teachers for not doing what you were meant to do. Part of being responsible is using your time wisely.

42. Setting Priorities and Avoiding Procrastination

Here is a list of activities. Place each activity in order, from the most important to the least important.

- Playing video games
- Hanging out with friends
- Eating dinner with your family
- Playing sports after school
- Exercising
- Doing your chores
- Studying
- Doing your homework
- Helping your parents when they ask
- Watching a movie
- Eating sweets after dinner
- Visiting the park

- Reading a book

Sometimes, the things you love doing are not as important as some of the things you hate. That may cause you to *procrastinate*. Procrastinating is when you avoid doing things that are important by wasting time doing unnecessary things. You should always make sure that you do the important things that you do not like before you do anything you find enjoyable.

Organizing your time by deciding what is more important is a straight path to success. People who have achieved great things know that their attention should be on one thing at a time. Writing a list of everything you need to finish for the day and then ordering it according to what is most important is a great way to make the most out of your limited time. Arranging a list like this shows you what matters in your life, and you can cut away the things that waste your time if you fall behind on what you need to complete in a day.

43. Creating Schedules

Planning your day can help you do everything you need to on time.[12]

Planning your day can help you do everything you need to on time. There are different daily tasks you do, like sleeping, washing, eating, school, and chores. Ask your parents or an adult for some help. There are 24 hours in each day. Below is a space for each hour. Write down what you will do in each hour from Monday to Friday.

Hours	Task	Completed (Yes/No)
00:00-01:00		
01:00-02:00		
02:00-03:00		
03:00-04:00		
04:00-05:00		
05:00-06:00		
06:00-07:00		
07:00-09:00		
09:00-10:00		
10:00-11:00		
11:00-12:00		
12:00-13:00		
13:00-14:00		
14:00-15:00		
15:00-16:00		
16:00-17:00		
18:00-19:00		
19:00-20:00		
20:00-21:00		

21:00-22:00		
22:00-23:00		
23:00-00:00		

Here is an example of how your daily planner could look:

Hours	Task	Completed (Yes/No)
00:00-01:00	Sleep	Yes
01:00-02:00	Sleep	Yes
02:00-03:00	Sleep	Yes
03:00-04:00	Sleep	Yes
04:00-05:00	Sleep	Yes
05:00-06:00	Sleep	Yes
06:00-07:00	Get Ready/Breakfast	Yes
07:00-08:00	Leave for School	Yes
08:00-09:00	School	Yes
09:00-10:00	School	Yes
10:00-11:00	School	Yes
11:00-12:00	School	Yes
12:00-13:00	School	Yes
13:00-14:00	School	Yes
14:00-15:00	School	Yes

15:00-16:00	Soccer Practice	No (Season Over)
16:00-17:00	Homework	Yes
17:00-18:00	Screen Time	Yes
18:00-19:00	Dinner	Yes
19:00-20:00	Bath/Shower	Yes
20:00-21:00	Sleep	Yes
21:00-22:00	Sleep	Yes
22:00-23:00	Sleep	Yes
23:00-00:00	Sleep	Yes

You can make one of these schedules for each day of the week. So, you will have seven schedules from Monday to Sunday.

Goal-Setting and Planning

Goals are the things in life that you wish to achieve. For example, you may have a goal of getting an A in math class. Setting goals guides your life in the direction that you want it to go.

44. SMART Goals

Setting goals is a process that you need to think carefully about because they will help you decide how you spend your time. That is why SMART goals can be very helpful. SMART stands for Specific, Measurable, Achievable, Relevant, and Time-bound.

- **Specific:** Your goals have to be described in detail. For example, you will get an A in math.
- **Measurable:** For goals to be measurable, there has to be a way to measure your progress. You cannot just say my goal is to try harder in math. How will you know if you've tried hard enough? For example, you can set that goal by aiming to get an A.
- **Achievable:** The goals you set should be realistic. For example, you cannot say you will become a professional soccer player by next year. It takes a lot of time to become a professional, and you are too young to play at that level. Your goals must be reachable.
- **Relevant:** Your goals must be relevant to you. Imagine if you set a goal to become a better hockey player, but you hate hockey and do not play it. That would be very silly.
- **Time-Bound:** You have to set a time limit for yourself in order to stay motivated. For example, you will get an A in math *by the end of the year.*

Ask your parents or an adult for help. Write down some goals using the SMART method.

45. Action Plans

After setting some goals, you can make a plan on how you can achieve them. For example, if you want to get an A in math or any other subject, your action plan could include getting extra lessons after school, paying more attention in class, and studying for an hour before you go to sleep.

Ask an adult to help you draw up an action plan to achieve the goals you set for yourself in the previous exercise.

Adaptability

Adapting is when things *aren't* going according to plan, so you make changes. Imagine playing a fighting video game against your best friend. You keep trying the same moves that helped you against other people, but he keeps beating you. To win, you will have to change moves or pick a new character.

46. Adjusting Your Plans

Sometimes, you make a plan to achieve your goal, and it does not work. Maybe you are getting a C in math class. You make a plan to study an hour a day because you want an A, but you still end up getting a C. That means you have to change your plan. Sometimes, it can feel like you have let yourself down because your plan did not work. Beating yourself up will not get you to where you want. Don't look at having to change your plans as a sign of failure. Instead, think of the adjustment as a part of the process. Making changes just means you are so dedicated to winning that you are willing to question yourself and grow despite mistakes.

When things do not go according to plan, ask yourself:

- Why is the plan not working?
- What information are you missing?
- What changes can you make to the plan?
- Which of your past plans failed?
- What could you have done to change your plan and improve it?

47. Dealing with Barriers

A barrier is something that stops you from achieving your goal. Barriers make people give up. To be successful, you cannot quit at the first sign of trouble. You must find ways to get over them and achieve your goals.

- Write down a goal you have.
- Write down some of the things stopping you from reaching it.
- Now, think of how you can make changes to overcome those challenges.

Stress Management

Stress is the feeling you get when you are worrying about things in your life. Too much stress can be very unhealthy, so it is extremely important to find ways to deal with it.

48. Meditation

Meditation is an activity you can do to reduce your stress. The way meditation works is by bringing you into the present moment so your mind is clear, and you do not have to worry about the past or the future too much.

Meditation is an activity you can do to reduce your stress.[13]

Here is a simple meditation activity you can try when you feel stressed:

Sit with your legs crossed and your back straight. Close your eyes and breathe in and out slowly. Count each breath while focusing on your breathing. Take 100 breaths. Try it and see how you feel afterward.

49. Asking for Help

You are growing up, so you want to do things on your own. You are very capable of doing a lot of things, but everyone needs help every once in a while. If you are stressed or struggling, remember that you can always ask a friend, a teacher, or your parents for help.

Lebron James is one of the best basketball players in the world. No matter how good Lebron is, if he steps onto the court alone to play against another team, he will definitely lose. His greatness is only as good as the supportive team he has around him. It is good that you want to better yourself, but it is impossible to do it without the help of others.

Think of something you have been struggling with. Go and ask someone for help and see how the problem gets solved.

Section 6: Money Management

A long time ago, people used to hunt animals, collect plants to eat, and make tools and clothes. Eventually, they learned how to farm so they could raise their own animals and grow the plants they needed to survive. People used to trade their animals, plants, and the products they made in a system called bartering. As time went on, people started using money to buy what they needed instead of trading goods.

You need money to survive. Your parents or caregivers pay for most of what you need and may even give you some spending money if you behave. When you grow up, you will have to buy everything you need yourself. If you use your money wisely, you can make even more and buy all the things that you wish. If you do not know how to manage your money well, you will end up wasting it.

When you finish school, you will either find a job or study further to learn a skill that you can use to make money. Some children get part-time jobs to make money while they are in school. Others might get money to do chores around the house. *Money does not fall out of the sky.* The only way to make money to buy the things you want is if you work hard and use it wisely.

Coins and Currency

The United States uses dollars. Paper money is called *notes*. There are seven different types of notes: $1, $2, $5, $10, $20, $50, and $100. You also have coins including 1 cent, 5 cent, 10 cent, 25 cent, 50 cent, and $1. 10 cents is a dime, a nickel is 5 cents, a penny is 1 cent, and a quarter is 25 cents.

The process of buying and selling products and services between people is called the economy.[14]

100 cents is equal to one dollar. People set prices for the goods or the services they offer. The reason people sell products is to make a profit. If it costs a person $50 to make a teddy bear, they will sell it for more than $50. The profit is anything over the amount the product or service costs. So, if a teddy bear costs $50 to make and the owner sells it for $70, the profit is $20. To work out the profit, you must subtract the selling price from the costs.

The process of buying and selling products and services between people is called the economy. When the economy is good, everyone will have enough money to buy the things they need. However, when the economy is bad, some people will struggle to make enough money.

50. Working with Different Notes and Coins

You can add up different combinations of coins and notes to make different values. For example, two 50-cent coins are the same as a $1 note, or two $20 notes and a $10 note are the same as one $50 note.

Here are some simple sums using coins and notes. Write down the value of each sum using one note or coin.

Example: 50 cents + 50 cent = $1

25 cents + 25 cents =

$50 + $50 =

25 cents + 25 cents + 25 cents + 25 cents =

$10 + $10 =

50 cents + 25 cents + 25 cents =

51. Paying for Stuff and Getting Your Change

When you go to the store to buy things you want, like toys or candy, you will use notes or coins. Sometimes, you will not have the exact amount of money you need to pay. If you have too little, you will not be able to buy what you want. If you have too much money, you can still buy the product, but the store owner will need to give you some back, which is called change.

If an item costs $5 and you have a $10 note, the store owner will give you $5 back.

Calculate the change you will get in the following scenarios:

- An apple is $5, and you have $10. How much change will you get?
- A candy bar is 25 cents; you have 50 cents. How much change will you get?
- A new TV is $50; you have a $100 bill. How much change will you get?
- A shirt is $25, and you have $50. How much change will you get?
- A pair of shades is $15, you have $20. How much change will you get?
- A packet of chips is $1.75, you have $2. How much change will you get?

Wants and Needs

The things people buy fall into two groups: wants and needs. Wants are the items or services that people buy but can live without. Needs are the things that people buy because they need them to live, like food, clothes, houses, and electricity. Before you can buy anything you want, you must first make sure that all your needs are met. Your needs must be the first things that you spend money on. If you have money left over, you can save some or spend it on what you want.

Right now, your parents or caregivers are the ones who provide most of your needs. One day, you will be responsible for taking care of your own needs and wants, and maybe even the needs of others. Therefore, you must understand how needs are met and what they are. Figuring out what falls into the group of wants and what falls under needs is a big step to becoming more responsible and independent.

52. The Difference Between a Want and a Need

Understanding the difference between a want and a need will help you manage your money a lot better. Wants are nice to have, but you can live without them. You might have a lot of things that you want to spend money on, but you can't afford to buy everything. You have to figure out the best way to spend your money by working out what you need and what you can do without.

Now that you understand how needs and wants work, you should be able to group products into the categories of needs and wants. Sorting goods into the categories of needs and wants is the first step to understanding how society uses money to function. Below is a list of a few products you can find at a local market. Sort all of these products into either a want or a need.

- Vegetables
- Meat
- Ice cream
- The Internet
- A video game
- An action figure
- A skateboard
- A car
- A household
- A toothbrush
- Toothpaste
- Clothing
- A bed
- A gold watch

A scented candle Needs:

Wants:

53. Budgeting

Workers have to use their salary each month to buy all the things they want and need. For people to make sure that they spend their money in the right way without wasting any, they draw up a plan of exactly what they will spend their money on. This plan is called a *budget.*

To make a budget, you will add up your entire salary, which is the money you get paid weekly or monthly for working. You will then take your salary and compare it to what you want and need. After you calculate how much your wants and needs cost, you will use the money you earn to pay for them. If you do not have enough money, you will either need to cut some things out that you want to buy, or you will have to find ways to make more money. Budgeting is an important skill to have because you will manage your money better so that you can take care of yourself and others.

You have $500. Below is a list of products you can spend your $500 on. You can spend your money on whatever you like, but remember to save some of it as well.

- A pair of shoes: $20
- A t-shirt: $15
- A pair of shorts: $15
- Ice cream: $5
- Chocolate: $5
- Vegetables: $10
- Steak: $20
- A toy car: $475
- A video game console: $499
- A yoyo: $20.
- School books: $50.

Now answer the following questions:

1. What did you use your $500 on and why?
2. How much money do you have left to save?
3. Did you remember to first use your money for what you need before buying the things you want?
4. How much spending money do you get?
5. What do you use your money on, and how much of your spending money do you save?

Earning and Spending Money

Money always flows because people are always earning and spending money. There are many ways to make money in the world and even more ways to spend it. Think about how many advertisements you see in a day. There are billboards, radio ads, posters, and video ads on YouTube. They all show you the different products that people are selling. People have the choice to spend their money on the many products that are out in the world. Just because there are many great things to buy does not mean that you should spend your money on every unnecessary item you see.

54. How to Earn Money

Your parents may give you money as a gift because they want to be nice to you. This will not always happen. To get money, you need to work. If you are lazy, you will never make money to buy the things that you want and need.

Ask your parents or caregivers about their jobs. Ask them if they like working and if it is difficult. Your parent's answers may surprise you, and it will show you the hard work it takes to earn money.

People exchange their time for money. They go to college or teach themselves new skills so that they can get jobs that pay them more money.

As you are still being looked after by your caregivers, they buy you all the things you need, like school supplies, clothes, and food. They also pay for the home in which you live. One day, you will need to earn money to buy everything you need for yourself. What job would you like to do to earn money?

You could do some things to earn money right now, like doing chores, selling candy and water, or even selling arts and crafts that you have made yourself.

Ask your parents what you can do around the house or in the yard in exchange for money. Don't forget to ask them how much they will give you.

55. Spending Your Money Wisely

Once you have earned money, you must find ways to use it wisely. The best things to buy after you have taken care of all your needs are products that can make you more money. For example, you might buy paint and paper to make artwork that you can sell.

- Can you think of more stuff to buy that can help you make more money?
- You never want to use all of your money. You need to save some of it to use later.
- How much money have you earned this week?
- What will you use your money on?

Saving

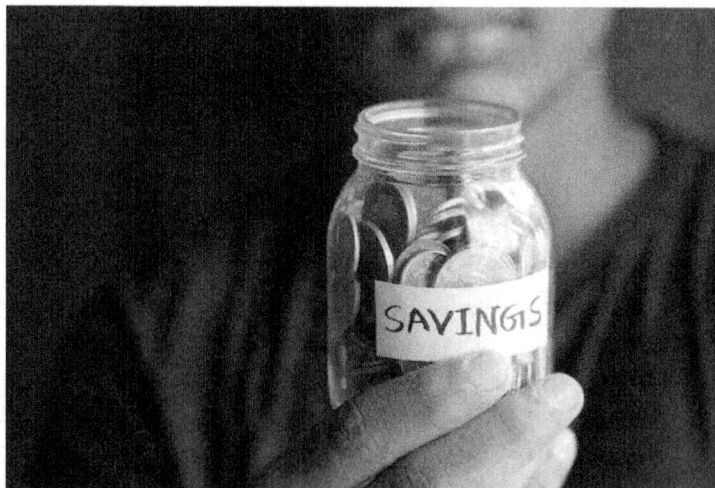

Saving is when you have some money left over at the end of the week or month, and you put it to one side.[15]

Saving is when you have money left over at the end of the week or month and put it to one side. If you save your money over a long time, you will be able to buy something bigger. For example, if you save $10 every month for 12 months, at the end of the year, you will have $120. People save their money to buy big items that they cannot afford immediately.

People also save their money for emergencies. For example, a rough storm might break a piece of someone's roof off. If they did not plan and save money in case of emergencies, they might not be able to fix their roof.

Saving your money is a great habit to have. People who waste their money do not have enough when they need it. If you have enough saved, you can help your friends and family when needed. Spending your money as soon as you get it is fun at the moment, but you will regret it when you find something that you really want. You can buy candy now or put aside money and wait for a little bit. Maybe saving your money will pay for the toy or video game that you've been begging your parents for.

56. Bank Accounts

Bank accounts are where people put their money to keep it safe. If you kept all your hard-earned money under the mattress, someone might break in and steal it. A bank is much safer.

There are two main types of bank accounts: a checking account and a savings account. A checking account is what people use every day to access their money. A savings account is where people save money. There is also the credit card. People use it to borrow money from the bank. On a credit card, people spend money they do not have, but they have to pay the bank back with a little bit extra added on called interest.

Ask your parents if they can open a savings account for you at the bank to put money into until you are 18.

57. Saving for a Rainy Day

Saving for a rainy day means putting money away for emergencies. You might put aside $10 every month that you never touch unless something bad or unexpected happens.

Can you list some emergencies that you think people would need to save for? An example would be a medical emergency, like breaking an arm.

Financial Goals and Planning

Rich people know exactly what they want to do with the money they have, and they make plans about how to get more in the future. For you to use your money wisely, you must make detailed plans with the money you earn. Making financial goals is a great way to manage your money. For example, a financial goal will be something like saving to buy a bicycle after a year or two.

58. Thinking about the Future

- Is there anything you would like to buy in the future?
- Can you research how much that item costs?
- How much money are you earning at the moment?
- How much of that money are you able to save?

- If you save that amount every month, how long will it take you to afford the item?

You should ask questions like these whenever you are thinking about how you will use your money in the future.

59. Making Plans with Money

- What are your plans for the money you earn or the spending money you get?
- Why do you want to spend your money on that?
- Is there anything you are saving for?
- What would be the most responsible way to spend your money?

Before you spend even one cent of your money, you should know exactly what you want to do with it and think about how it can benefit you now and in the future.

Section 7: Household Chores

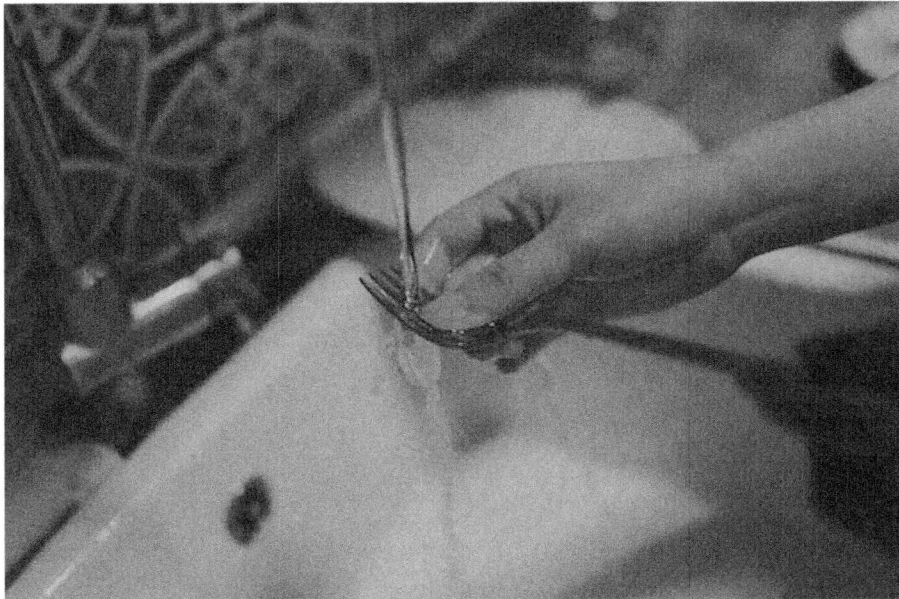

Household chores are part of everyday life, ensuring everything within the home remains organized, accessible, and clean.[16]

Household chores are part of everyday life, ensuring everything within the home remains organized, accessible, and clean. Regular tasks like cleaning, cooking, and organizing contribute to maintaining cleanliness and promote the overall health and safety of the entire family. Understanding your responsibilities and actively participating in house chores is part of being a productive family member. It's all about working together, helping each other, and making home management more achievable for everyone.

Before exploring the skills revolving around household chores, you need to understand why they're necessary and the difference they make in life.

Being Responsible

Part of being responsible is taking care of your personal belongings, like toys, gadgets, books, etc. Taking matters into your own hands and fulfilling them responsibly will prepare you to take on bigger responsibilities later in adulthood.

Independence

Learning a new skill and mastering it provides a sense of accomplishment. You'll become more self-sufficient, rely less on your family, and be ready for life's challenges.

Time Management

Taking up chores around the house improves your time management skills, which are crucial as you juggle school, activities, and social commitments.

Organization

When you perform household chores, you'll foster the planning and organization skills necessary for your future endeavors. Learning and implementing organization skills will also provide relief and boost your self-esteem.

Work Ethic

Developing a solid work ethic is crucial if you want to achieve success in whatever you do. The process will make you understand the value of hard work and relish the satisfaction achieved after finishing tasks.

Teamwork

While certain household chores like organizing your room or caring for pets can be done individually, several chores, such as vacuuming the home, maintaining the garden, or tending to guests, are a team effort. Giving a hand in these tasks will teach you teamwork and improve communication skills.

Problem-Solving

When doing chores by yourself, you may encounter an issue or a challenge. When put in a challenging situation, your brain starts thinking of creative solutions, improving your brainstorming and problem-solving.

Resource Appreciation

You'll be developing an appreciation for the resources required to maintain a home; this helps you learn to use other resources responsibly, too.

Empathy

Doing chores can show you the efforts others put into maintaining a household, increasing your empathy towards people, and developing gratitude.

Living Independently

Learning to clean, cook, and do essential home maintenance work is vital for independent living. Practicing these chores early on will make your independent life easier, especially when you leave home for college.

Household chores are not just a matter of keeping your home clean and organized. They are a vital part of family life, teaching responsibility and life skills and fostering unity. By sharing these tasks and working together, you not only maintain your home but also build strong, supportive relationships that can last a lifetime.

Understanding the significance of these chores and their impact on life is the first step toward becoming a responsible and capable family member. Through these tasks, you learn various life skills that extend beyond the home and into your future endeavors, from maintaining good hygiene and time management to honing problem-solving and teamwork abilities.

60. Cleaning Your Bedroom

A clean and organized room is an excellent space to relax, rest, play, or do homework. Whether preparing your bed or organizing your toys or gadgets, it's your responsibility to keep everything in place; after all, it's your bedroom.

Decluttering Your Bedroom

Start by collecting clothes around the room and putting them in the laundry basket. Clean clothes can be hung up neatly in the wardrobe. Likewise, start collecting garbage like pieces of paper, plastic wrappers, or anything else that should be thrown away. If plates or cups are in the room, take them to the dishwasher.

Making Your Bed

When making your bed, use a fresh set of linen daily and change the entire bedding at least once a week.

Dusting the Room

Use a microfiber cloth to remove residual dust on tabletops, desks, or surfaces you can easily reach. You can also assist family members with vacuuming. Having food in your room regularly will attract bugs. Make it a food-free zone and make it a habit to eat in the dining area or the kitchen.

61. Cleaning the Office or Study Room

When studying, you'll inevitably find yourself surrounded by loose papers, writing tools, and books. Get rid of loose papers, store your pens and pencils neatly, and organize your books.

Cleaning your space can help you focus better.[17]

62. Preparing the Night Table (Nightstand)

Most of the time, the night table is a dumping ground for whatever you do before bed. Whether reading a book, listening to music, or using a gadget, always clean the night table when you're making the bed in the morning. Items you commonly use before bedtime, like accessories, books, or gadgets, can be stored inside the drawers.

63. Organizing Your Closet

Closets can quickly become the least organized space if you don't regularly pay attention. At least once every six months, go through your closet, organize it, and dispose of anything you no longer use. If you feel there's less space to hang clothes, ask parents or guardians to install a shelf or rails. The items you tend to use the most should be placed in the closet where you can easily reach them. Don't hesitate to ask for help from a family member if you are still confused about organizing the closet.

64. Cleaning Windows

Glass surfaces should be cleaned with a microfiber cloth and a mild cleaning solution. You must spray the solution all over the window glass and wipe it with a cloth until all streaks and dirt are gone.

Maintaining Good Cleaning Habits

Each chore related to room cleanliness and organization will take some time to get the hang of. When you do, make them a part of your daily routine.

A simple list will include chores like making the bed, putting away toys, gadgets, clothes, etc., in their respective places, and cleaning up garbage. To take it even further, you can even create a weekly cleaning routine to allocate specific days for chores. For example, you can allocate Saturday for vacuuming and dusting, Sunday to organize the closet, Monday to take out trash, and so on.

65. Washing Dishes

First, make sure you are wearing dishwashing gloves, as certain chemicals in cleaning products can cause skin dryness, irritation, or itching, especially in people with sensitive skin. Most households nowadays have dishwashers, eliminating the time and manpower required to wash dishes and kitchen utensils. Still, it's necessary to learn the old-school methods of washing dishes manually, as these skills come in handy during outdoor adventures or when living somewhere without a dishwasher.

Prep the Sink

Before you start, clean the sink from plates, utensils, leftover food, or scrapings. Doing that prevents sink clogs.

Fill the Sink

You'll see a stopper or a shut-off valve near the sink tap. Fill the sink with lukewarm water and add dishwashing soap to form a mild soap solution.

Soak the Dishes

Immerse dishes, cups, glasses, and utensils in the soapy water, soaking them for at least five minutes. Letting the dishes sit in soapy water makes removing grease and food residue clinging to the surface easier.

Washing

Use a sponge to wash dishes, glassware, cups, and utensils gently. Use a scrubber for greasy and hard-to-clean surfaces like a frying pan, and pay extra attention to areas with residue.

Rinse

Unclog the sink when you wash, letting the soapy water drain. Now open the tap and hold dishes under running water or make a basin of clean water for rinsing.

Drying

You can use a clean washcloth or stack things on a drying rack to let them air dry.

Special Care

Be extra cautious and gentle when washing glassware. Always hold a glass from the base, not the top or stem, to prevent slipping while washing. For effective cleaning, use a non-abrasive scrubber for pots and pans with stubborn stains. Using a standard scrubber can scratch the non-stick surface (Teflon) on some pots and pans – so ask a parent or guardian how to clean those special items.

Preparing and Serving Daily Meals under Supervision

66. Preparing Meals

Wash your hands thoroughly with soap and warm water before handling any food. This is a crucial step in maintaining good hygiene while cooking. If you're new to cooking, start with simple recipes like sandwiches, salads, or scrambled eggs. These are easy and safe options for beginners.

When you're ready to cook, carefully read the entire recipe before you start. Pay attention to ingredients, measurements, and instructions. Always have an adult supervise or assist when using the stove, oven, or sharp knives. These appliances and tools can be dangerous if not used correctly. Always write down the cooking times and temperatures for the recipe you are making, and use a timer to avoid overcooking, burning, or undercooking the food.

67. Serving Meals

Before you start plating and serving food, take a quick look at the table. Make sure it has clean plates, glasses, napkins, and other utensils. Arranging the table before cooking is best as you won't have much time during preparation. Plate the food and serve it to the guests. You can also ask the guests politely whether they want any condiments or seasonings before eating. When plating, always pay attention to the portion size and keep it the same. To maintain cleanliness in the kitchen, clean up as you go along and wash utensils, dishes, and the tools used for cooking.

68. Vacuuming and Sweeping Floors

Vacuuming Floors

Unwind the vacuum cleaner's power cord and plug it into the outlet. Turn it on and adjust the setting according to the type of flooring you're cleaning. Keep it steady during the vacuum cleaning process and make overlapping passes to ensure thorough cleaning. If you notice it's not sucking up debris properly or that the bag is almost full, switch the vacuum off and empty the bag into the trash.

Some vacuum cleaners have disposable bags, whereas others have canisters that must be cleaned thoroughly and placed back in. Follow the manufacturer's instructions when emptying and cleaning vacuum bags. Be careful of cords to prevent tripping.

Sweeping Floors

A broom and a dustpan are all you need to remove dirt and debris from floors. No matter the type of broom you use, just make sure the bristles are not worn out; otherwise, dust can cling to nooks and corners. Start sweeping from one corner of the floor, piling it up slowly, and keep doing that until you reach the other end. Use the dustpan to scoop everything up. After emptying it, give the floor a final sweep to pick up the remaining dust or debris.

69. Caring for Pets

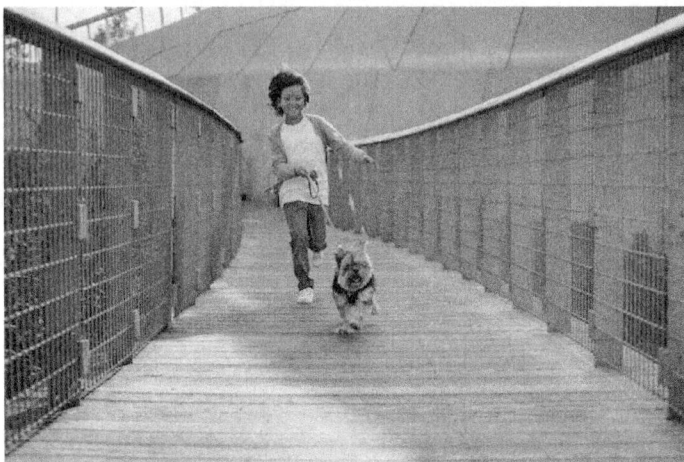

No matter whether you have a cat, dog, or guinea pig, every animal needs some form of playtime or exercise.[18]

Feeding

Always follow a feeding schedule for your pet. Besides portioning food and following a schedule, make sure they have access to clean and fresh water around the clock.

Cleaning

If you have a pet using litter boxes or cages, follow a cleaning schedule.

Exercise

No matter whether you have a cat, dog, or guinea pig, every animal needs some form of playtime or exercise. Make it a priority to play with your pet daily for a set amount of time. For example, if you have a dog, you can take them for daily walks, or if you have a cat, provide interactive toys to provide them with mental and physical stimulation.

Healthcare

Keep a close eye on your pet's health. You should keep a record of their vaccinations and schedule vet checkups as recommended. If you notice any red flags, immediately contact the veterinarian. Besides taking care of their health needs, keep your pet groomed as it promotes health. A basic grooming routine includes trimming the nails, cutting fur, and bathing.

Safety

Always handle your pet gently and with care. Be attentive to their body language to understand their emotions and needs. Approach them calmly and avoid making sudden movements that might startle them.

Responsibility

Taking care of a pet is a significant responsibility. Make sure you're ready to commit to their needs before getting one – and remember *they depend on their owners for love, care, and attention.*

ADDITIONAL HOUSEHOLD CHORES:

Here are some more household chores you can learn:

Lawn Care

Under the supervision of a parent or guardian, learn how to operate a lawn mower and trim the grass. In the fall, gather and bag leaves from the yard. Remove weeds from flower beds and the lawn. Take care of watering the garden or potted plants as needed. During the winter, clear the driveway and sidewalk of snow.

Sorting and Washing Clothes

Learn to separate laundry by color, fabric type, and washing instructions. Load clothes, add detergent, and set the appropriate wash cycle. After washing and drying, try folding and organizing clean laundry items.

Making a Shopping List

Assist in creating a grocery list based on the household's needs. Accompany an adult to the grocery store and select items from the list. Put away groceries when you return home.

These chores contribute to the cleanliness and organization of your home and provide valuable life skills and responsibilities that will serve you well in the future. Remember to ask for guidance and supervision when learning new tasks, especially those involving equipment or tools. For example, you'll need supervision when helping out in the kitchen or grocery shopping with family. It will take some time to get accustomed to these household chores. While some may catch your interest more than others, remember that learning every household chore will benefit you in the future.

Understanding the significance of these chores and their impact on life is the first step toward becoming a responsible and capable family member. Through these tasks, you learn various life skills that extend beyond the home and into your future endeavors, from maintaining good hygiene and time management to honing problem-solving and teamwork abilities.

You should also recognize that taking on household chores isn't just about personal development but also about *contributing to the overall well-being of your family.* By working together and sharing these responsibilities, you not only ensure the smooth functioning of your home but also build strong, supportive relationships with your family members and anyone else you'll live with in the future.

As you become more proficient in these tasks, you'll be better equipped to adapt to new challenges and responsibilities that life may throw your way. The lessons you learn while helping with household chores will serve you well in college, at the workplace, and in your personal life.

Remember, it's perfectly normal to take some time to get used to these chores, and it's okay to seek guidance and supervision when learning new tasks, especially those involving potentially hazardous equipment or tools. The important thing is to approach these responsibilities with a positive attitude, recognizing that they are stepping stones towards becoming a capable and responsible adult. So, embrace these chores, learn from them, and enjoy the sense of accomplishment that comes from taking care of your home and family.

Section 8: Safety First – First Aid

Safety awareness is all about staying proactive, vigilant, and ready to deal with the risks you could face in everyday life. It begins with sharpening your ability to recognize and identify potential hazards in your surroundings.

Safety awareness is all about staying proactive, vigilant, and ready to deal with the risks you could face in everyday life.[19]

These hazards include anything like your school corridor's wet floor or a sharp object like scissors lying on the kitchen counter unattended. Your actions can influence the outcomes, saving you and others from accidents or injuries. For example, you can safely put the scissors in their designated drawer or walk slowly down that slippery corridor. In both cases, safety awareness is about identifying hazards and taking the proper steps.

This chapter will familiarize you with safety measures like traffic rules, first aid techniques, fire safety, etc.

Recognizing Risks

Safety awareness begins with the identification of potential hazards in the environment. It can be anything like a slippery floor, a sharp object, loose wires, etc., creating unsafe conditions. Knowing about these risks and identifying them on time is the first step toward safety awareness.

Understanding the Implications

Any unsafe action you perform can have potentially adverse outcomes. Neglecting safety measures and being reckless will only result in an injury or accident. It can even escalate to a life-threatening situation when not appropriately dealt with.

Preparing Yourself

Another critical aspect of safety awareness is anticipating the potential outcomes after identifying hazards. It also involves knowing what actions you need to take and their importance. Actions like knowing that a person should look both ways when crossing the street or understanding the importance of wearing safety gear when riding a bike.

Staying attentive and vigilant makes identifying these hazards and developing an effective action plan much easier. Lastly, acting responsibly can aid significantly in keeping you safe. Not eating in the classroom or following traffic regulations are some other examples. While learning about safety awareness empowers you to take the proper steps and act responsibly in various situations, it also contributes to a safer environment for the entire community.

70. Traffic Safety Practices

When crossing the street, always look both ways for coming traffic. Don't forget to use crosswalks and follow pedestrian signals. Follow relevant traffic rules and regulations. Whether you're on a scooter, skateboard, or bike, there are rules set by local authorities that you need to adhere to at all times. If you cannot find these rules online, ask your parents or teachers for help. Remembering and complying with traffic safety practices contribute significantly to protecting you and the people around you.

71. Fire Safety Practices

You must know the location of fire exits and escape routes in your school and home. While you won't find any sign in your home, fire exit signs in public places and schools guide you toward the safest escape route in case of a fire. Also, avoid playing with flammable materials like matches and lighters.

Attending fire safety drills is the best way to learn more about fire safety. Most schools arrange drills so you can better understand these hazards and know the safety measures to take. However, if you are home-schooled or have missed these fire drills, you can always go with your family and ask the local fire department if they have any classes or drills you can attend. Most schools, public places, and even homes nowadays have a fire extinguisher. Knowing its location and using the information you learned from fire safety drills can keep you safe.

72. Water Safety Practices

Learning how to swim is a universal skill that may come in handy. The best way is to ask your parents or guardians to arrange for a swimming instructor. In a pool, always follow the set rules. Likewise, it's best to wear a life jacket when boating or playing other watersports, especially if you haven't learned to swim.

73. Stranger Awareness

Be vigilant outdoors and cautious around strangers. If someone offers a treat, ride, or an offer, politely refuse. Avoid sharing your credentials or any form of personal information with a stranger. This also includes people you interact with online. Keeping your credentials from falling into the wrong hands protects you from identity theft. It may not be much of a concern now, but you will learn to appreciate how important this is when you grow up.

74. Internet Safety

Always use unique and strong passwords for your accounts. When interacting with people, never share your personal information. You should also report inappropriate online behavior and share your concerns with a trusted adult for guidance. When browsing the internet, use it responsibly and avoid exploring websites that seem unsafe. Install antivirus software that comes with malware and internet protection.

75. Bullying Awareness

While having fun and being open to interactions is great for learning, knowing about abusive behaviors and taking preventative steps at the right time is also necessary. If you experience or have witnessed bullying, immediately report it to a family member, teacher, or school counselor, as this toxic behavior should always be discouraged.

76. Kitchen Safety

Under adult supervision, you can learn knife-handling skills like cutting, holding, and using the cutting board.[20]

Under adult supervision, you can learn knife-handling skills like cutting, holding, and using the cutting board. Before jumping right into chopping vegetables and cooking, it's better to help out family members in the kitchen and serve guests to familiarize yourself with kitchen etiquette and related skills. You can ask a family member to teach you about operating the stove, the hazards involved, and the safety measures to take.

77. Home Alone Safety

When alone at home, don't open the door before you know who is on the other side. Always take your time and identify the person. If it's a stranger, don't open the door and notify a trusted adult. You can ask your parents or caregivers to prepare a list of emergency contacts, including the contact number of a trusted neighbor, in case you need help.

78. Nature Safety

Outdoors, be cautious around wild animals, and never approach or feed them. When camping or hiking, always follow a plan and be prepared to adapt in case the weather changes. As most outdoor adventures will be with your family, helping them during preparation and following their lead can be a great learning opportunity.

79. Bicycle Safety

When riding a bike, wear the necessary safety gear like knee pads and helmets to prevent injuries in case of falls or accidents. You should also be familiar with the traffic rules for biking in your area.

Calling for Help

While following rules and safety measures can, most of the time, ensure safety, there are certain situations where you must call for assistance. That includes medical emergencies, severe accidents, and injuries. The way you will call for help may change, depending on the situation. For example, immediately inform your parent or caregiver about the situation if you are at home and your sibling gets injured while playing.

If you are alone at home, immediately grab the phone and call your local emergency response service. You can ask a family member to write down emergency contact numbers or search them online and note them down so you know who to call during an emergency.

First-Aid Basics

Learning first aid basics instills valuable and potentially life-saving knowledge and skills that can be effective in medical emergencies, injuries, and accidents. Whether you're at home or out on the field playing, accidents can occur anywhere. Knowing the steps to take prevents injuries from worsening and, in some cases, can even save lives. Besides learning about the basics, it's crucial to have confidence, be prepared, and responsibly tend to the medical emergency, especially during critical situations.

Contents of a First-Aid Kit

Adhesive Bandages

Adhesive bandages cover minor cuts, abrasions, or blisters, providing an antiseptic effect and reducing exposure to harmful microorganisms. Clean the wound or injury site with an antiseptic wipe or solution and pat it dry before applying the bandage. Now, carefully place the antiseptic patch of the bandage on the wound and press the edges firmly to secure it.

Sterile Gauze Pads

When the injury is deep, sterile gauze pads can prevent bleeding. These pads can also be used as a dressing, effectively covering wounds that cannot be covered with an adhesive bandage. Just as with adhesive bandages, clean the injury site with an antiseptic solution or wipes and place a sterile gauze pad over it. Now cut some adhesive tape and secure the gauze pad's edges, ensuring it stays in place.

Adhesive Tape

It's simply a tape used to secure gauze pads and wound dressings. You will mainly use adhesive tape to secure gauze pads during wound dressing.

Antiseptic Wipes or Solution

Antiseptic wipes or solutions contain chemicals that kill germs and prevent infections.

Tweezers

Tweezers come in handy when applying a dressing or to remove foreign objects from the skin, like thorns and splinters. Before using tweezers, disinfect them using an antiseptic solution or wipe.

Scissors

Scissors in your first aid kit are meant to cut gauze pads or remove clothing from the injury site. Before using them, disinfect them with an antiseptic solution to minimize the spread of germs to the injury site.

Disposable Gloves

Wear disposable gloves when providing first aid. They prevent the germs on your hands from contaminating the injury site and decrease the chances of infection. After giving first aid, dispose of the gloves properly. First aid kits contain biohazard plastic waste bags, which should be used to dispose of gloves. Use a regular plastic bag if a biohazard waste bag is unavailable. Avoid throwing the plastic waste bag outdoors and only send it to a waste disposal facility dealing with biohazardous waste.

OTC Medications

Several over-the-counter (OTC) medications, including pain relievers, are in a standard first aid kit. Acetaminophen and ibuprofen are common pain relievers that reduce minor pain and fever. Keep in mind that they won't effectively reduce the pain caused by severe injuries or accidents. Other medications include anti-diarrhea, antacids, laxatives, cough and cold medications, antiseptic ointment, etc. Knowing the dosage of each medication is also necessary to avoid overdoses and their effects. If you have a problem remembering the dosage, write it down on paper and put it in the kit for future reference.

Emergency Blanket

A shiny paper-like blanket that provides insulation, keeping the body warm in case of exposure to freezing weather or when someone experiences shock.

Emergency Contact Information

Make a contact information list containing numbers of emergency hotlines, local hospitals, medical assistance services, and family members that can be reached during an emergency. You or someone else can use the contact information to call in help accordingly.

The first aid kit's contents can change depending on its use. For example, a first aid kit for hiking and outdoor adventures will have different contents from the kit at home. Most kits include a content manual. You can always refer to the manual if you ever need help remembering something. Don't hesitate to ask your parents if you are unsure about how to use something.

Wound Care Basics

Materials Needed

- Surgical or disposable gloves
- Antiseptic solution or wipes to clean the wound
- Adhesive tape
- Sterile gauze pads or adhesive bandages
- Scissors

Step 1: Wash Your Hands

Start by washing your hands thoroughly with soap and water for at least 20 seconds.[21]

Start by washing your hands thoroughly with soap and water for at least 20 seconds. This ensures that your hands are clean before treating the wound. If available, consider wearing clean, disposable gloves to prevent contamination. However, if you are outdoors with no access to water or soap, use a sanitizer or wear the sterile gloves you find in the first aid kit to prevent further contamination.

Step 2: Stop the Bleeding

If the cut or scrape is bleeding, apply gentle pressure with a clean cloth or sterile gauze pad. Maintain pressure until the bleeding stops, which usually takes a few minutes. Elevating the injured area can also help reduce bleeding.

Step 3: Prepare for Cleaning

Before cleaning the wound, gather all the necessary materials, including antiseptic wipes or solution, sterile gauze pads or adhesive bandages, adhesive tape, and scissors. Everything required should be within your reach as you want to minimize the chances of wound contamination.

Step 4: Clean the Wound

Use an antiseptic wipe or solution to clean the wound. Gently wipe around the injured area, starting from the center and moving outward. Do not scrub the wound, as this can damage delicate tissue. Use a new wipe or clean section of cloth for each pass to avoid spreading dirt or bacteria.

If debris or foreign material is visible in the wound, use sterile tweezers. Always grasp the foreign material as close to the skin's surface as possible.

Step 5: Apply an Antiseptic

After cleaning, apply a thin layer of antiseptic ointment or cream. This prevents infection and supports the healing process. Make sure the antiseptic covers the entire wound.

Step 6: Cover the Wound

For more minor wounds, place an adhesive bandage over the clean, antiseptic-treated area. The adhesive bandage should fully cover the wound without wrinkles. Apply a sterile gauze pad over the antiseptic-treated area for slightly larger wounds or scrapes. Use adhesive tape to secure the gauze pad in place. Apply the tape so that it firmly holds the gauze in position but does not stick directly to the wound.

Step 7: Check for Allergies

If the person with the wound is known to be allergic to adhesive materials or certain antiseptics, consider using hypoallergenic options like sterilized gauze and paper tape.

Step 8: Monitor and Change Dressing

The time it takes for a wound to heal depends entirely on how well you care for it. Your aim should be to keep the wound as clean as possible. Open wounds and deep injuries require daily cleaning and dressing changes. Regularly check the wound for signs of infection, such as redness, swelling, pus, or increased pain. Change the dressing whenever you notice any of those signs.

Step 9: Seek Medical Attention When Necessary

If the wound is deep, won't stop bleeding after applying pressure, shows signs of infection, or is located in a sensitive area (face, genital area, etc.), seek medical attention as soon as possible. Bleeding from the wounds on limbs can be stopped using a tourniquet or by wrapping a piece of cloth tightly above the site of the wound. Tying it slows down the blood flow to the wound, increasing the chances of blood clotting, which is the body's process to prevent bleeding. Changing the dressing of deep and infected wounds must be done by a certified healthcare professional as they will not only clean the wound appropriately but also monitor it and change the course of treatment as necessary.

Step 10: Properly Dispose of Materials

Safely dispose of used gloves, antiseptic wipes, and other contaminated materials in a sealed plastic bag. Wash your hands thoroughly after removing gloves.

Proper wound care prevents infection and supports the body's natural healing process. Following these detailed steps, you can effectively clean and dress minor cuts, scrapes, and burns, promoting a quicker and more comfortable recovery.

Section 9: Empathy and Compassion

Empathy is when you put yourself in another person's shoes to understand their feelings. Compassion is when you feel for someone. When people have no compassion and empathy, they can be very mean and rude. If someone trips and falls, having empathy means that you should help them up. If you don't have empathy, you will just laugh at them. How would you feel if everybody laughed at you if you fell? Just as you do not like being laughed at or hurt, other people don't either.

Empathy is when you put yourself in another person's shoes to understand their feelings.[22]

To have compassion and empathy, you must think about how what you do makes others feel. When your parents or caregivers ask you to tidy up your room or to clean the mess you made, and you do not do it, they can get angry. Your parents work hard, so when you ignore them, it hurts their feelings. If you think about others and how they feel, you could clean up before your parents even ask you. This is how compassion and empathy can make your home life easier.

In the same way that empathy is important at home with your family, thinking about the feelings of others can also help you make friends. If you were mean and heartless to all the people you met, they would never want to spend time getting to know you. When you treat people well, they will respond by being nice to you, too. Empathy, respect, and compassion all lead to you being treated positively. Any relationship you have with friends and family can only get stronger when you show that you care with your words and actions. You cannot just say that you love somebody; you must show it.

Understanding Your Emotions

To recognize other people's feelings, you must first be able to understand your own. Feelings happen automatically, so you might not think about how they pop up. It can be difficult to control how you feel because it just happens, but you can control how you act when you have a certain feeling. You are meant to be the master of your emotions, so how you feel should not be able to control what you do.

80. Describe Your Emotions

Sometimes, you do not have the words to describe what you are feeling. Different things make people feel bad. What is okay and fun for you might make your friend feel terrible. You have to be able to communicate exactly how you feel because some people will not know whether you are fine with their behavior or if what they are doing is bothering you.

Those who cannot describe or understand their emotions can act out in unacceptable ways, like hitting or hurting people. To prevent yourself from acting in ways that you will regret, the best thing you can do is learn to feel and explain your emotions. When you have a deeper understanding of what is going on inside your body and mind, it will be easier for you to control yourself. Self-control is one of the most important traits you can have to be successful. You are the boss of your feelings. They should never be in charge of what you do.

Explaining what is happening in your mind and body when you are feeling something is a great way to understand your emotions better. For example, if you feel angry, your body might get hotter, and your muscles might feel stiff.

Describe how the following emotions feel inside your body and mind:

- Happy
- Sad
- Excited
- Frustrated
- Tired
- Lonely
- Angry
- Disappointed

81. Controlling Your Feelings

Once you can describe how you are feeling, you are in a better position to control your emotions. Just because you feel bad does not mean you should take your feelings out on other people, especially if they did nothing wrong. To act with empathy means that you must be aware of your emotions while also considering how you are making the people around you feel.

Imagine that someone has given you a brand new T-shirt as a gift. The T-shirt has a character you love on it, and it is your favorite color as well. The first time you wear it, a friend accidentally spilled some soda on it. They apologize and try to clean it up, but they end up just making it worse.

Draw a picture of the worst response you can have, one that does not consider your friend's feelings.

Now, draw another picture of a response you can have that shows some empathy and compassion.

Which of these two responses that you drew do you think will help you become better friends? Mistakes happen, and sometimes, people are *truly sorry* for what they did. Part of empathy is the ability to forgive and respond in ways you control your emotions without having an outburst or throwing a tantrum.

Having Empathy and Compassion

The main point of empathy is to be less selfish and think about what others are experiencing. People will not always say how they are feeling, so you will have to look at their facial expressions or their body language. If someone is sad, their shoulders might be slumped, and their head will be down. If someone is frustrated, they might scratch their head and rub their eyes a lot. To fully understand someone and how they are feeling, you must listen to them and look at how they are behaving. Paying attention can help you have more empathy and compassion. Just like you must put in some effort to understand your emotions, you will need to put in even more work to understand the feelings of other individuals.

82. Imagine Yourself in Their Shoes

- Can you think of the last time you and your sibling or best friend had a big fight or argument?
- What was the argument about?
- Who started it, and how did it end?
- Draw a comic book strip of the argument with different panels showing the whole fight.
- Imagine that you were your best friend or sibling.
- How do you think they felt?
- Why do you think they acted the way they did?

Putting yourself in someone else's shoes can help you understand the bigger picture of why they say and do certain things.

Draw a picture of a better way you could have dealt with the argument that would have respected everyone's feelings and made sure that everybody walked away happy.

83. Helping People

Have you ever struggled with something so long that you almost gave up until somebody showed you how to do it? Nobody can go through their whole life without help. When you help people, you will feel good inside, and they will be more willing to help you when you need it. Collaboration means working together for a common goal. When you collaborate with different kinds of people, you will find that you are great at some activities and not so much at others.

1. Think of a friend or family member that you can help.

2. What do you think they will need help with?

3. How can you help them?

4. Draw a picture of you helping someone you love.

5. Draw a picture of yourself helping someone in need.

Are you up for a challenge? See how many people you can help this week. Help as many people as possible and see how you feel like a superhero by the end of it.

The Golden Rule

What are some of the rules that you have to follow at home or school?

Can you guess what the golden rule is?

The rule that everybody should remember is to treat others how you want to be treated. Before you say or do anything to somebody, always stop to think about whether you would like it if someone did the same thing to you. If someone makes you so angry that you want to punch them, stop and ask yourself if you would like it if someone punched you. When you treat others how you want to be treated, you spread kindness and make the world much better to live in.

84. Recognizing the Value of Others

People are special. Everyone has something unique and good to offer the world. To increase your empathy, you must realize that you are valuable and precious, but so is everybody around you. The way you want to be treated is how you must treat others.

Since you want your feelings respected, you must think about how your actions make people feel. You must also consider that emotions can change the way people act and what they want from you. If someone is angry, they may want to be left alone, or if a person is happy, they will be open to playing with you. Putting yourself in the shoes of other people can help you to build stronger relationships.

- Who is your favorite person in the world?

- Why are they your favorite person?

You are also somebody's favorite person, and people that you do not like are loved by others. Everyone has value, even if you do not see it immediately. If you treat people like trash, they will behave like trash, but if you treat them like diamonds, they will shine so bright you will have to squint your eyes.

Write down the names of five people you like. Next to their names, write down what makes them special and why you appreciate them.

85. Being Grateful

Being thankful can help you see all the positivity in the world.[23]

Being thankful can help you see all the positivity in the world. Being grateful and thanking people for everything they do for you will make you a much happier person, and it will also make their day because they know you appreciate them.

Write a list of ten things that you are grateful for.

_____

_____

_____

_____

_____

_____

_____

_____

_____

_____

Now, write a list of ten people you are grateful for.

_____

_____

_____

_____

_____

_____

_____

_____

Why are you grateful for these people?

_____

_____

_____

_____

_____

_____

_____

_____

_____

_____

_____

Giving thanks is not only polite, but it is a great way to express love and care for others. Make sure you say thank you as often as you can.

Think Before You Act

People can make horrific decisions because they let their emotions rule them, and they do not think before they act. You have an intelligent brain, so you can use it in the right way. To have empathy, you must think about what you do or say to others. Acting recklessly is not good for you and is definitely bad for the people around you. When you do not think before you act, you put other people and yourself in danger. That's why you need to calm down, take a breath, and think before you act. You also have to think about your actions after you do something negative so you can find ways to correct yourself and be better in the future.

86. Slow It Down

You do not always have to rush to make a choice. Slow down and think about what you are doing. Acting just because you feel forced or pressured, even by your own mind, can lead you into a lot of trouble. There is always a better way to do the right thing, but you will never know what it is if you do not stop and think.

There are decisions that you can make without thinking a lot about them, like whether you want a green or a blue balloon. This choice does not have a big impact on your life. Other choices that you make have heavier consequences. The responsible thing to do is to slow down before making a major move. A lot of mistakes are made because people rush and jump into the deep end. Slowing yourself down allows you to process better so you can avoid making unnecessary mistakes or walking down the incorrect path.

Before you do anything, stop and ask yourself:

- Is this the best decision you can make right now?
- Can doing this hurt you or others?

Taking a few deep breaths or walking away from a stressful situation can also help you think better. You have time to slow down and make the right choices to make sure that you do not hurt yourself and others.

87. Actions Have Consequences

Everything you do has consequences. Those can be positive or negative. For example, if you punch someone, the consequence of that could be them punching you back even harder. If you get good grades in school, the consequence of that could be a reward from your parents or caregivers.

- What are the consequences of calling someone a rude name?
- What are the consequences of hugging a friend when they need it or ask for it?
- What are the consequences of making your parents a sandwich?
- What are the consequences of playing with sharp knives?

Every action will result in something positive or something negative. To be happy, you must think about the consequences of your actions before you do them. If you play ten hours of video games every day instead of studying, you are likely to fail your test. If you put the work in, you will pass with flying colors. The actions you take today will affect the person you become tomorrow. Before you make any decision, think about whether it is leading you to a bright future or down a dark and miserable road. Some things are fun in the present, but in the long term, they can affect you if you do not think about the consequences of your actions.

Bullying

Bullying is when you hurt someone with your words or actions, especially if they are weaker than you. When you bully someone, you are not showing empathy because you harm the person without considering their feelings. Bullying can cause people to be miserable and can even make them want to hurt themselves. If you see someone getting bullied, you should stop it by telling a teacher or an adult. If your friends are bullying someone, do not join in. Instead, call them out on it.

88. How to Identify and Stop Bullying

There are a few ways to identify if bullying is happening to you or other children.

If you see someone who is always hurt, like they've got bruises and cuts all the time, they may be getting bullied.

When people play mean jokes or call you rude things, it is bullying.

If you find yourself afraid to go to certain places because you are avoiding someone, or if you want to sit alone, you might be getting bullied.

If you feel uneasy around someone, it could be a sign that they are bullying you.

If your friends are nervous or scared around certain people, they may be being bullied by them.

If you see or experience any of these signs, speak to a trusted adult like your teacher or parents.

89. Steps to Take If You Are Being Bullied

If someone is bullying you, there are a few steps you can take to stop it.

The first thing you could do is to tell the bully that you do not like what they are doing and would like them to stop.

If they do not stop, you should tell an adult.

Stay away from the places where the bullies hang out.

Stay in big groups so bullies do not target you.

Remember, bullying is unacceptable, so you cannot allow it to happen to you or other children.

Section 10: Dealing with Failure

When you are faced with failure, what is the first emotion you experience? Fear? Frustration? Regret? What about pride, determination, or satisfaction? These emotions are often associated with success. When you attach them to failure, you will realize that they are as naturally fitting as the missing pieces of a jigsaw puzzle.

Without failure, there can be no success. Failure isn't a hurdle you have to jump over. It is a step you need to climb on your way to success, a trail on the mountainside that leads to its peak. You may stumble and fall the first time around, but you will get back up again and use it to reach the top.

All those who have succeeded today have failed at some point in their lives.[24]

All those who have succeeded today have failed at some point in their lives. The only difference between them and other people is that they learned from their failures and carried on. Did you know that J.K. Rowling's Harry Potter manuscript was rejected 12 times? Today, she is among the most successful authors in the world, with more than 500 million books sold around the world.

Then there is Steven Spielberg, who directed soul-stirring movies like *Saving Private Ryan* (1998) and *Schindler's List* (1993). He failed to get a place in a film school during his college years, not once but twice in a row! Albert Einstein was deemed a failure right from birth. While most children learn to speak at the age of two, Einstein didn't utter a single word until he was four years old. He couldn't read until he was seven, and he had to take his father's friend's help to land a meager job as a clerk at the Swiss Patent Office. Despite all his failings, his theories of relativity, quantum mechanics, and light became a turning point in the world of astrophysics.

At your age, failure can be academic, athletic, or personal. Academic failure is when you fail to achieve the required grades. Athletic failure is when you fail to win a sports competition. With time and effort, these two forms of failure can easily be overcome. After all, the goals here are set by society (your school and the sports administration). When you fail to achieve them, it doesn't hurt much.

Personal failure, on the other hand, can hurt like the worst kind of pain. When you fail to meet your own expectations, you may be at a complete loss for words. You may feel dazed and flustered, like a sparrow fluttering around in a closed room, looking for a way to escape. You may be completely lost, not understanding what to do next.

The answer is simple. Lower your expectations. That doesn't mean lowering your self-esteem but setting achievable goals for yourself. After any failure, when you achieve a personal win, you will feel much better about yourself than just winning outright. A person who has developed a habit of winning takes their achievements for granted. But if you have succeeded after a string of failures, you will understand the true value of that win, be it personal, academic, or athletic.

There is a professional failure as well, which you will experience a few years down the line. If you know how to deal with your failures at this age, handling future professional failures will be a breeze.

90. Failing Forward

Failing forward is a belief that helps you embrace failure as a force that pushes you toward a bright future. Failure takes you one step back so you can gain the momentum to leap several steps forward. You should accept this belief to be able to fail forward. Otherwise, you will always remain one step behind.

To experience this force and leap ahead, you need to learn from your failures. Imagine it as a teacher with a hands-off teaching style. You stumble and fall, but failure doesn't help you back up. It shows you how to help yourself up. Write down the mistakes you made that led you to fail. Avoid making them again the second time. Adapt your strategy as the situation demands. Take note of your positives, too, so you can repeat them or improve your technique.

91. Resilience

Resilience is your ability to endure hard times and eventually bounce back from them. Take yourself back to the first time you failed at something. You may have felt like nothing would ever go right for you. How long did that feeling last? Then, the next time you failed, did it last a little longer? That marked your growing resilience to failure. The more you fail, the more resilient you become, and the easier it will be for you to transform a bad situation to your benefit. Success won't be too far behind once your resilience starts growing.

92. Growth Mentality

Your penchant for growing, regardless of the severity of the situation, defines the effectiveness of your growth mentality. Assume you hit a rough patch in your science project. You will need to dismantle the whole thing, find the mistake, fix it, and reassemble it again to successfully finish the project. The only way to move forward is to go back.

Many of your peers will just give up at this point or try their hand at another, easier project. If you have a growth mentality, however, you won't think twice before heading back to square one to embrace eventual success. For you, it's like jumping on a trampoline. You apply just a little more pressure downward to soar much higher than before.

93. Self-Compassion

How do you view yourself when you fail? What is your opinion of yourself? Do you tend to hate the person you have become? Do you look down on yourself? Each time you fail, you may be going through the same emotions. When you achieve your first success, you will start to question yourself: what was the point of being so hard on yourself? You could have been successful without hating yourself. That is exactly what self-compassion is.

It's the practice of treating yourself with the same love and care during failure as you would after your successes. It's the art of loving yourself unconditionally. Failure helps you develop this important trait, leading you to become happier and more optimistic in the future. Once you learn to be compassionate with yourself, negative emotions will haunt you less often, and you will learn to embrace failure like a long-lost friend.

94. Positive Self-Talk

Society labels failure as something negative. It looks at a failed individual like some dirt stuck on the heel of a shoe. Don't seek aid and encouragement from society to pull you back from your failures. Look within yourself. Start with some positive self-talk. Remember the voice you heard when you failed the first time? It was all negative, right?

What will your friends and peers think of you now that you have failed? What if you fail again? It will be worse than making a fool of yourself.

Instead, try to give a positive twist to your thoughts.

Failure is nothing but a challenge for you, a challenge to succeed. It has lent you the strength to go the extra mile to achieve your goals. It has made you more resilient, more worldly, and more experienced. You have gained the power to turn this failure into several successes.

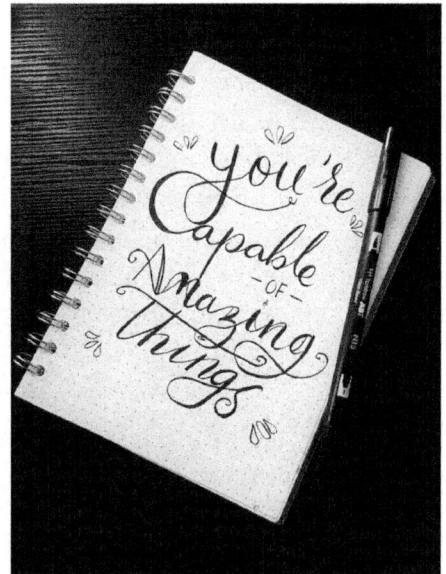

Start with some positive self-talk.[25]

95. Tackling Emotional Struggles

What did you feel when you failed? Sadness, frustration, and anger are common emotions that come with failure. Your first instinct will be to fight them. Don't. Feel them from the bottom of your heart. Let them wash over you. Accept that these emotions are a part of the healing process. However, take care not to spiral down into their murky depths. Once you have experienced the negative emotions, it's time to let them go with some positive self-talk.

Remind yourself that failure is an integral part of life's struggles. Only through failure can you hope to achieve success. It has the power to instill all the qualities that will make you successful. Don't expect to start experiencing positive emotions overnight. It is a slow process, and at times, it can go at a snail's pace. One day, you are sure to wake up feeling refreshed and ready to take on another round of failure to achieve success. That will be the day you will have tackled all your emotional struggles.

96. Solving Problems

Imagine an individual who has been encountering one success after another. They have never failed in their life. They have never faced any problems. They have read about ways to solve hypothetical problems, but they never experienced them in person. When such an individual encounters failure for the first time, they will be at a complete loss as to how to move forward. They may be left dumbstruck, like a child discovering the world for the first time.

You, on the other hand, have already had dealings with failure. You know how it feels, how devastating it can be. You have already encountered the problems that come with it. It has given you the strength to deal with those problems and the mental ingenuity to solve them. You have learned to think critically and approach a viable solution that can make problems go away.

97. Discovering Your Interests

At your age, you may already have a list of your favorite subjects. Say you like the world of science and its cold, hard facts. You love to come up with theories from something apparently insubstantial. You have a passion for devouring any scientific book you come across, including the school curriculum. Nevertheless, there may come a time when you fail to get good grades in the subject. That moment will show whether or not you are truly interested in science.

Will you get back up, analyze your failure, overcome your mistakes, and move forward? Or will you simply lose interest in the subject and start exploring something new? Failure helps you discover new and existing interests, gives voice to your passions, and shapes your future.

98.The Power of Foresight

When you failed for the first time, you may not have taken the possibilities leading to that failure into account. That's why it hurt so bad. Now that you have learned from it, you will not only work to succeed but consider the possibility of failure as well. You will also work to avoid that failure, giving you the power of foresight. You will have both the dos and don'ts in mind, and you will be prepared for any eventuality. If you fail again, it will be simply another learning curve for you. It's just another list of possibilities to add to your growing arsenal of foresight.

99. Handling Regrets

Regrets are an important part of failure. Without regrets, you won't have anything to learn from. They pave the way toward progress. They teach you to embrace failure and look forward to success. They improve your decision-making ability by showing you what's right and wrong, along with opening up the world of gray areas. They provide a sense of clarity in your goals and desires, shining a light on the path ahead. So, don't hesitate to feel regret for your failures, but with caution. Just as every coin has two sides, regrets come with their own set of drawbacks.

Regrets are an important part of failure.[26]

When you think too much about your regrets, you fail to appreciate the value of your failures. It leads to undue stress and lowers your confidence. You may also experience frustration and anger towards everything that led you to this point. When you dwell on your regrets, you don't learn anything from them. Your failures may haunt you day and night. Then, you will begin to see any failure not as a stepping stone toward success but as an unending spiral of negativity. Handling your regrets from failure is a life skill that will lead you to future success.

It goes without saying that the next time you see failure looming on the horizon, don't be afraid. It's just another landmark on your way to success, a stop-off point where you can assess your journey so far and plan for your future.

Thank You Message

Thank you so much for completing this book. You have worked hard and deserve all the praise in the world!

Remember that the work is not over. For this book to do its job, you must use the skills you have learned. Working on them every day helps you become your best at communicating, forming and keeping relationships, and being a great friend by showing compassion and empathy. On top of those valuable lessons, you have learned about how to work with people. You have also gained key skills like doing household chores, managing your money, and being safe.

These skills are useful both now and in the future. You can always revisit chapters when you are having trouble with a specific part of your life.

No one ever stops growing; we are always changing. When you find yourself having unfamiliar experiences, it can help you apply some of the skills you have gained here. Reading is not enough, so you must apply yourself and put all the exercises provided into action.

Good luck, stay positive, and enjoy yourself!

If you enjoyed this book, I'd greatly appreciate a review on Amazon because it helps me to create more books that people want. It would mean a lot to hear from you.

To leave a review:
1. Open your camera app.
2. Point your mobile device at the QR code.
3. The review page will appear in your web browser.

Thanks for your support!

Check out another book in the series

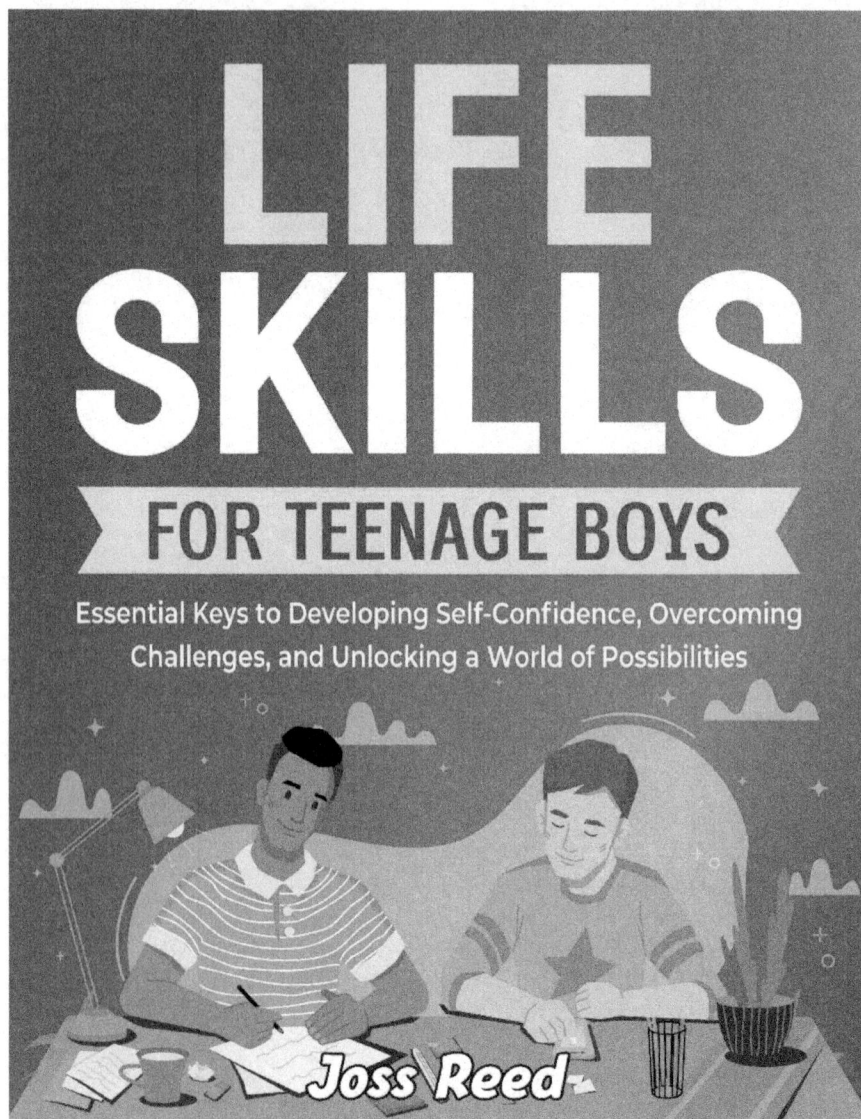

LIFE SKILLS

FOR TEENAGE BOYS

Essential Keys to Developing Self-Confidence, Overcoming
Challenges, and Unlocking a World of Possibilities

Joss Reed

References

(N.d.). Britishcouncil.org. https://www.britishcouncil.org/voices-magazine/how-help-teenagers-stay-safe-online

(N.d.). Edtechreview. In. https://www.edtechreview.in/trends-insights/insights/rational-thinking-a-skill-for-young-minds/

35 activities to teach respect. (2016, April 14). The Robert D. and Billie Ray Center. https://raycenter.wp.drake.edu/2016/04/14/35-activities-to-teach-respect/

5 public speaking tips to persuade any audience. (2021, August 3). Nest. https://www.latrobe.edu.au/nest/5-public-speaking-tips-to-persuade-any-audience/

American money. (n.d.). Usa.gov. https://www.usa.gov/currency

Amy Morin, L. (2010, September 8). Chores list for older kids and teens. Verywell Family. https://www.verywellfamily.com/over-50-ideas-of-chores-for-teens-2609291

BagayaK. (2022, January 6). 13 examples of good character. OpEx Managers; BagayaK. https://opexmanagers.com/examples-of-good-character/

Bendlin, E. (2020, October 21). Why children need chores. Nebraska Methodist Health System; Methodist. https://bestcare.org/news/why-children-need-chores

Betts, J. (2022, October 11). Teach kids how to clean their room without the stress. LoveToKnow. https://www.lovetoknow.com/parenting/kids/how-teach-child-clean-their-room

Bhasin, H. (2019, April 11). How to be honest? 14 ways to be honest and practice honesty. Marketing91. https://www.marketing91.com/14-ways-to-be-honest/

Bloggers, S. (n.d.). Helping kids understand the value of keeping promises. Bedtime Stories. https://www.storyberries.com/helping-kids-understand-the-value-of-keeping-promises/

Boogaard, K. (2021, December 26). How to write SMART goals. Work-Life by Atlassian. https://www.atlassian.com/blog/productivity/how-to-write-smart-goals

Bryant, C. D. (n.d.). What is good character? Talking with Trees Books. https://talkingtreebooks.com/teaching-resources-catalog/definitions/what-is-character-definition.html

Bullying: how to spot the signs in children and teenagers. (2022, November 25). Raising Children Network. https://raisingchildren.net.au/school-age/behaviour/bullying/bullying-signs

Crescentini, C., Capurso, V., Furlan, S., & Fabbro, F. (2016). Mindfulness-oriented meditation for primary school children: Effects on attention and psychological well-being. Frontiers in Psychology, 7. https://doi.org/10.3389/fpsyg.2016.00805

Currency and coins. (n.d.). U.S. Department of the Treasury. https://home.treasury.gov/services/currency-and-coins

Defining critical thinking. (n.d.). Criticalthinking.org. https://www.criticalthinking.org/pages/defining-critical-thinking/766

Dewar, G. (2020, August 22). Teaching empathy: Evidence-based tips for fostering empathic awareness in children. PARENTING SCIENCE; Gwen Dewar. https://parentingscience.com/teaching-empathy-tips/

Difference between checking and savings accounts. (n.d.). Santanderbank.com. https://www.santanderbank.com/personal/resources/checking-savings/difference-between-checking-savings

Ellis, R. R. (2023, January 4). Failure is actually good for kids. How you can get out of their way and foster their resilience. Fortune. https://fortune.com/well/2023/01/04/failure-is-good-for-kids-resilience/

Engler, B. (2022, September 2). Teaching your child to deal with conflict – connections academy®. Connectionsacademy.com; Connections Academy. https://www.connectionsacademy.com/support/resources/article/building-conflict-resolution-skills-in-children/

First-aid guide for kids: How to treat scrapes, cuts, minor burns and more. (n.d.). Optum.com. https://www.optum.com/health-articles/article/healthy-living/first-aid-guide-kids-how-treat-scrapes-cuts-minor-burns-and-more/

Flatley, K., & Certified Parent Educator. (2023, June 5). 70+ ideas for how to make money as a kid. Self-Sufficient Kids. https://selfsufficientkids.com/how-to-make-money-as-a-kid/

Fusco, K. (2019, July 18). 5 productive self-talk practices for working through failure. SUCCESS. https://www.success.com/5-productive-self-talk-practices-for-working-through-failure/

Germer, C. (2017, January 5). To recover from failure, try some self-compassion. Harvard Business Review. https://hbr.org/2017/01/to-recover-from-failure-try-some-self-compassion

Giving thanks can make you happier. (2021, August 14). Harvard Health. https://www.health.harvard.edu/healthbeat/giving-thanks-can-make-you-happier

Gleeson, B. (2020, August 25). 9 powerful ways to cultivate extreme self-discipline. Forbes. https://www.forbes.com/sites/brentgleeson/2020/08/25/8-powerful-ways-to-cultivate-extreme-self-discipline/?sh=1ef0934c182d

How often do children need to take a bath? (n.d.). Aad.org. https://www.aad.org/skin-care-basics/child-bathing

How to Use Active Listening Skills to Coach Others. (n.d.). Center for Creative Leadership. https://www.ccl.org/articles/leading-effectively-articles/coaching-others-use-active-listening-skills/#:~:text=Active%20listening%20requires%20you%20to,building%20block%20of%20compassionate%20leadership

Important life skills: 5 things to teach your children about failure. (n.d.). Edu.Kh. https://www.invictus.edu.kh/news/important-life-skills-5-things-to-teach-your-child-about-failure

Improve your child's active listening skills. (2017, June 13). Oxford Learning. https://www.oxfordlearning.com/improve-active-listening-skills/

Independent teens: 9 safety tips for going out alone. (2017, June 30). Shine365; Marshfield Clinic. https://shine365.marshfieldclinic.org/kids-health/independent-teens-safety-tips/

Johnson, A. (2018, May 17). 11 signs you're a bad friend —even if you think you aren't. Insider. https://www.insider.com/signs-youre-a-bad-friend-2018-5

Jones, K. (2023, March 20). Encourage students to ask for, and accept, help. Evidence-Based Education. https://evidencebased.education/encourage-students-to-ask-for-and-accept-help/

Kidscape. (n.d.). How to make new friends. Org.uk. https://www.kidscape.org.uk/advice/advice-for-young-people/friendships-and-frenemies/how-to-make-new-friends/

Kipman, S. (2014, September 10). 15 highly successful people who failed before succeeding. Lifehack. https://www.lifehack.org/articles/productivity/15-highly-successful-people-who-failed-their-way-success.html

Levaire. (n.d.). Michigan Psychological Care. Michiganpsychologicalcare.com. https://michiganpsychologicalcare.com/blog/self-care-for-teens.php

Lusinski, N., & Gagliano, S. (2018, June 11). 9 boundaries you should have in your friendships, according to experts. Bustle. https://www.bustle.com/life/9-boundaries-you-should-have-in-your-friendships-according-to-experts-9345200

Myers, R. (2019, October 14). Kids chores list by age: The ultimate list of age-appropriate chores. Child Development Institute. https://childdevelopmentinfo.com/chores/the-ultimate-list-of-age-appropriate-chores/

Norman, R. (2022, April 22). Self-care (& hygiene!) skills for little kids. A Mother Far from Home. https://amotherfarfromhome.com/self-care-skills-for-toddlers-preschoolers/

Pangilinan, J. (2023, February 28). 111 self-discovery questions to ask yourself while journaling. Happier Human; Steve Scott. https://www.happierhuman.com/self-discovery-questions/

Pedersen, T. (2016, January 21). Can you physically feel emotions? Psych Central. https://psychcentral.com/blog/emotions-are-physical

Perry, E. (n.d.). What is Self-Discovery? 10 Tips for Finding Yourself. Betterup.com. https://www.betterup.com/blog/what-is-self-discovery

Reynolds, N. (2022, March 9). 50 potentially life-saving safety tips every teenager should know. Raising Teens Today. https://raisingteenstoday.com/safety-tips-every-teenager-should-know/

Self-care and teenagers. (n.d.). Reachout.com. https://parents.au.reachout.com/skills-to-build/wellbeing/self-care-and-teenagers

Self-care skills for kids: Tips, resources, & printables. (n.d.). Andnextcomesl.com. https://www.andnextcomesl.com/p/self-care-skills.html

Sobel, A. (2020, March 24). The power of authentic generosity to strengthen relationships. Andrew Sobel; Andrew Sobel, Inc. https://andrewsobel.com/article/the-power-of-authentic-generosity-to-strengthen-relationships/

Spulber, D. (2023, September 20). The benefits of chores for kids: Beyond a clean room. Parents.App; All About Parenting, Inc. https://parents.app/parenting/education-learning/chores-for-kids-beyond-a-clean-room/a/

Stano, K. (2020, December 18). How to support a friend or loved one in need. Hallmark Ideas & Inspiration. https://ideas.hallmark.com/articles/care-and-concern-ideas/how-to-support-a-friend-or-loved-one-in-need/

Sue. (2023, May 23). How to teach your teen basic first aid - help your teens. Help Your Teens -. https://helpyourteens.com/how-to-teach-your-teen-basic-first-aid/

Teaching your child to respectfully disagree. (2014, June 30). Nicole Schwarz, LMFT; nicoleschwarz. https://imperfectfamilies.com/teaching-your-child-to-respectfully-disagree/

The Editors of Encyclopedia Britannica. (2023). Golden Rule. In Encyclopedia Britannica.

The importance of schedules and routines. (2020, June 1). ECLKC. https://eclkc.ohs.acf.hhs.gov/about-us/article/importance-schedules-routines

What kids can do. (2019, September 24). Stopbullying.gov; US Department of Health and Human Services. https://www.stopbullying.gov/kids/what-you-can-do

Image Sources

[1] https://www.pexels.com/photo/baseball-player-in-gray-and-black-uniform-running-163239//

[2] https://www.pexels.com/photo/boy-brushing-his-teeth-8762973/

[3] https://www.pexels.com/photo/photo-of-planner-and-writing-materials-760710/

[4] https://www.pexels.com/photo/black-man-talking-with-son-on-knees-6624304/

[5] https://www.pexels.com/photo/photograph-of-kids-with-hats-talking-with-each-other-8023628/

[6] https://unsplash.com/photos/assorted-color-ninjago-plastic-figures-CXDw96Oy-Yw

[7] https://www.pexels.com/photo/close-up-photo-of-a-student-reading-a-book-5288652/

[8] https://www.pexels.com/photo/be-kind-lettering-on-white-surface-4439458/

[9] https://unsplash.com/photos/row-of-four-men-sitting-on-mountain-trail-TkrRvwxjb_8

[10] https://www.pexels.com/photo/boy-holding-dog-415100/

[11] https://unsplash.com/photos/do-something-great-neon-sign-oqStl2L5oxI

[12] https://unsplash.com/photos/closeup-photo-of-ballpoint-pen-near-camera-18mUXUS8ksI

[13] https://www.pexels.com/photo/a-boy-meditating-in-the-forest-8968261/

[14] https://unsplash.com/photos/10-and-one-10-us-dollar-bill-SAYzxuS1O3M

[15] https://unsplash.com/photos/a-man-holding-a-jar-with-a-savings-label-on-it-0ITvgXAU5Oo

[16] https://unsplash.com/photos/person-washing-fork-hQOHDAibf6A

[17] https://unsplash.com/photos/clear-spray-bottle-9gzU1mtTzWM

[18] https://www.pexels.com/photo/happy-ethnic-boy-running-on-bridge-with-cute-dog-5733432/

[19] https://www.pexels.com/photo/security-logo-60504/

[20] https://www.pexels.com/photo/a-man-in-black-long-sleeves-wearing-face-mask-while-slicing-a-steak-8477293/

[21] https://unsplash.com/photos/person-in-white-shirt-washing-hands-Ks4RTBgQ_64

[22] https://unsplash.com/photos/black-and-white-printed-textile-vVSleEYPSGY

[23] https://unsplash.com/photos/person-holding-white-and-black-i-love-you-print-card-fs_l0Xqlc90

[24] https://unsplash.com/photos/text-UN4PadDppAU

[25] https://unsplash.com/photos/pen-on-youre-capable-of-amazing-things-spiral-notebook-6GZQo28ecoE

[26] https://unsplash.com/photos/a-person-standing-on-top-of-a-mountain-Ijx8OxvKrgM

Printed in Dunstable, United Kingdom